▶▶▶▶▶▶▶ Cinema One

11 Pasolini on Pasolini

1

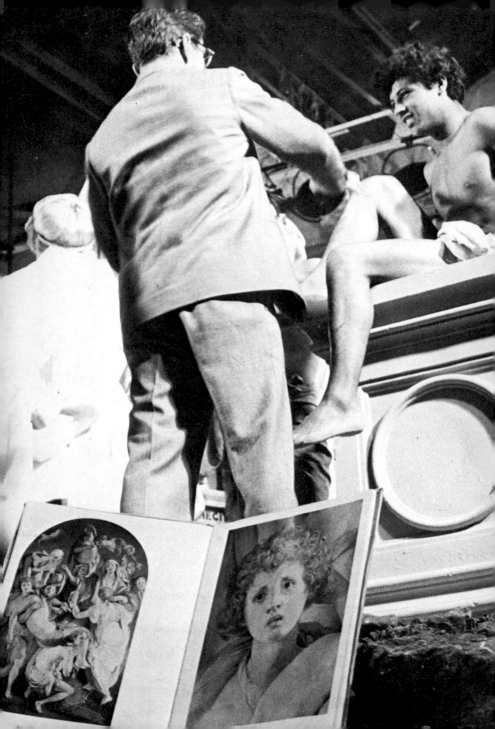

Pasolini on Pasolini

Interviews with Oswald Stack

PASOLINI, Pier Paolo (handwritten)

London

Thames and Hudson in association with the
British Film Institute

The Cinema One Series is published by
Thames and Hudson Limited
30–34 Bloomsbury Street, London WC1
in association with *Sight and Sound*
and the Education Department of the
British Film Institute, 81 Dean Street, London W1

General Editors
Penelope Houston and Tom Milne (*Sight and Sound*)
Peter Wollen (Education Department)

Pasolini on Pasolini by Oswald Stack
first published by Thames and Hudson 1969
is a publication of the British Film Institute
Education Department

500 47011 1 (hardcover)
500 48011 7 (paperback)

Designed by Bentley/Farrell/Burnett

Printed in Great Britain by
Jarrold & Sons Limited, Norwich

Contents

Pasolini in Palestine with Don Andrea Carraro; and as actor (High Priest) and director in *Oedipus Rex*

Introduction

Pasolini's cinema is deeply embedded in Italian culture: hence the confusion which many British and American critics have felt when confronted with his work. This is not only because many of the important influences on Pasolini – Pascoli, Gramsci, Rossellini – are little known here, but also because Italian culture itself is full of contradictory traits and components, which Pasolini's films reflect. The most obvious of these contradictions, of course, is that between Catholicism and marxism, the two commanding ideologies which dominate Italian intellectual life, both of which have left their stamp on Pasolini. The restlessness and eclecticism of Pasolini's career, which has shifted incessantly from one genre to another – painting, poetry, criticism, short stories, novels, feature films, reportage and now theatre – and from one style and subject-matter to another, reflects a search for some appeasement of the multiplicity of incompatible contradictions which have formed his view of the world and of art. Pasolini's marxism is far from being a unifying system: in his thought it is but one of many conflicting strands, now surfacing, now submerging.

If there is one constant, one invariant, it is Pasolini's uncritical attachment to the peasantry, an attachment which can be presented in the light of marxism, but more consistently in the light of a backward-looking romanticism. Pasolini first began writing poetry in Friulan dialect, under the influence of Giovanni Pascoli, on whom he wrote a thesis. But while Pascoli, who died in 1912, was writing before the First World War, Pasolini was writing after the Second. His Friulan poems are anachronistic, a rearguard action. But it was while he was in Friuli that Pasolini started to read Gramsci. He took from Gramsci the unorthodox 'Italian' elements of his thought: in particular, the emphasis on the potentially revolutionary role of the Italian peasantry and the need, in Italian conditions, for a 'national-popular' movement. Thus Pasolini was able to absorb marxism partially without permitting it to confront in their totality other aspects of his thought.

However, this heavily Gramscian version of marxism led Pasolini away from the hermetic, aristocratic circles in which his career had begun into the radical, left-cum-marxist cultural world which exists under the general hegemony of the Italian Communist Party. This is not quite the same as becoming a communist, or even a marxist. In most European countries Communist Parties have tended to adopt an *exclusive* approach (usually demanding some kind of formal submission to party directives). But in Italy, the Communist Party, under Togliatti's leadership and since, opted for an explicitly *inclusive* approach. To some extent this is a legacy from the Popular Front period. But it is also the product of the peculiar Italian cultural situation, where there is no lay culture which corresponds to the pervasive liberalism of the Anglo-Saxon countries. There is marxism (and its penumbra) and there is Catholicism (and its penumbra). The relationship between the Communist Party and a cultural personality such as Pasolini, or Visconti, for instance, is one of great flexibility on both sides. Thus Pasolini both writes for Party journals and at the same time, attacks the Party in non-Party publications.

When Pasolini started directing films he had already worked on a number of scripts, for directors like Fellini and Bolognini. This was on the strength of his Roman novels, *Ragazzi di vita* and *Una vita violenta*. Many of his scripts were set in the same Roman sub-proletarian milieu and these lead directly on to his first films as director, *Accattone* and *Mamma Roma*, which should be seen as part of his 'Roman' period including novels, scripts and films, as well as in conjunction with his later work as director. It is misleading to divorce Pasolini's work in the cinema from his other work, particularly his writing: poetry, novels, criticism. Like Robbe-Grillet and Kluge, Pasolini was a writer before he was a film director and his writing continues unabated: *Theorem*, for example, has appeared as a book as well as a film.

After *Mamma Roma*, Pasolini's next major work was *The Gospel According to St Matthew*, in which the influence of Rossellini, especially *Francesco, Giullare di Dio*, first became prominent. Pasolini's cinema is clearly in the tradition of Rossellini, Dreyer and Mizoguchi, if only in its juxtaposition of natural and supernatural, though it lacks the purity and coherence of the work of these masters. In *The Gospel*, for instance, a traditional Christology, drawn from sacred music and painting, is superimposed on the brusque and literal, Rossellinian treatment of a popular and anecdotal text. The result is to deliver the film into the hands of the Catholic Church. Yet *The Gospel* is the film of Pasolini which least betrays his drive towards eclecticism and pastiche. In *Uccellacci e Uccellini* different levels and styles, references to Rossellini, Fellini, Lukács, Togliatti, the Pope, and so on and so forth, jostle against each other in hopeless confusion.

Yet, despite the lack of any consistent drive, either in form or content, one underlying tendency can be discerned in Pasolini's career. He lays increasing stress on the need to restore an epic and mythological dimension to life, a sense of awe and reverence to the world: a sense which, he believes, the peasantry still sustain, though the bourgeoisie has done all in its power to destroy it. This emphasis on the spirituality of the peasantry, their semi-pagan consciousness of super-natural meanings and forces, is obviously difficult to reconcile with a marxist political analysis. In fact, rather than politics, it is sex which Pasolini now seems to see as the main threat to the bourgeoisie. In *Theorem*, it is sex which destroys the bourgeois family, its values and style of life. Moreover, by associating sex with pagan mythology – the groundwork for this was achieved in *Oedipus Rex* – and pagan mythology with the peasantry, Pasolini is able to reconcile the idea of sexual liberation with his attachment to the peasantry. This reconciliation, no doubt, will prove as precarious as others he has achieved in the past: it is difficult to believe that Pasolini's restlessness is now at an end.

These interviews were conducted in Rome over a period of two weeks in 1968. The original Italian has been edited in the translation. Pier Paolo Pasolini, who does not speak English, consented to the interviews being published in translation without himself checking the final version as printed here.

1: Background

You've written quite a lot about the importance of your family: could you tell me something about your early life and education?

My origins are fairly typical of petit bourgeois Italian society: I am a product of the Unity of Italy. My father belonged to an old noble family from the Romagna, while my mother comes from a Friulan peasant family which subsequently became petit bourgeois; my maternal grandfather owned a distillery; my mother's mother was Piedmontese, and she had Sicilian and Roman relations: so there is something from almost every part of Italy in me – but petit bourgeois Italy, I would stress, in spite of my father's noble blood. My early childhood followed this pattern as well: I don't have a home. I lived all over the place in Northern Italy. After I was born (in Bologna), I spent a year in Parma, then I went to Conigilano, then to Belluno, Sacile, Idria, Cremona and several other towns in the North.

It's rather difficult to talk about my relations with my father and mother because I know something about psycho-analysis, so I am not certain whether to talk about them simply in terms of poetic, anecdotal memory or whether to talk about them in psycho-analytical terms – which anyway I'd find rather hard to do, because, as you know, the last person to know oneself is oneself. What I can say is that I had a great love for my mother. You can check this in a series of poems, starting from about 1940 and going

Oedipus Rex: 'I always thought I hated my father'; and 'I had a great love for my mother' – Pasolini with Silvana Mangano in clothes copied from old photographs of Pasolini's mother

right up to the last book I wrote three or four years ago (when I gave up writing poetry).[1] For a long time I thought the whole of my erotic and emotional life was the result of this excessive, almost monstrous love for my mother. But quite recently I've realized that my relationship with my father was very important too. I always thought I hated my father, but in fact I didn't hate him; I was in conflict with him, in a state of permanent, even violent, tension with him. There were many reasons for this, the main one being that he was overbearing, egoistic, egocentric, tyrannical and authoritarian, although at the same time extraordinarily naïve. Besides, he was an army officer, and therefore nationalistic; he supported fascism, so this was another objective and quite justified reason for the clash. Moreover, he had a very difficult relationship with my mother. I only understand this now, but he probably loved her too much, and then perhaps this was not reciprocated fully, which kept him in a state of violent tension, and so, like all children, I sided mostly with my mother.

I always thought I hated my father, but recently when I was writing one of my latest verse plays, *Affabulazione*, which deals with the relationship between a father and son, I realized that basically a great deal of my erotic and emotional life depends not on hatred for my father but on love for him, a love which I had within myself when I was about one and a half years old, or perhaps when I was two or three, I don't know – at least that's how I have reconstructed things. My father died in 1959, after returning from a prisoner of war camp in Kenya. I dedicated a book of poetry which I wrote in 1942 in Friulan dialect to him. Friulan is my mother's dialect and obviously my father was against it both as an Italian coming from Central Italy who consequently in a somewhat racist way considered that anything that came from the margins of the country and had to do with dialects was inferior, and also as a fascist (because ideologically fascism was hostile to dialects, which were a form of real life it wanted to conceal). So it was quite a bold gesture to dedicate this volume of poetry to him.

13

How old were you when you began to feel what religion was? Did it come more from your family or from school?

My father was not a religious man, and he didn't believe in God. But as he was a nationalist and a fascist he was, naturally, conventional, and so he used to take us to Mass on Sunday for 'social' reasons. My mother, since she belongs to a Friulan peasant family, consequently a family with a religious tradition, but one which is absolutely natural and has nothing conformist or bigoted about it, never goes to church or communion: her religion is purely poetic and natural, which is something that comes mainly from her grandmother whom she was very fond of when she was a child. So my childhood was completely lacking in religious education. I think I am the least Catholic of all the Italians I know – I was never even confirmed,[2] and I always ran away from catechism lessons; I hated going to schools run by priests. Later I went to lay state schools and the Galvani *liceo* in Bologna was very important for me: this has a lay tradition and all my teachers there were laymen. So altogether religion at school had very little influence on me. I consider myself lay and non-believing. My religion is of a fairly atypical kind: it doesn't fit into a pattern. I don't like Catholicism because I don't like any institutions. On the other hand I feel it would be rhetorical to declare myself a Christian – although, as Croce said, no Italian can say he is not a Christian, culturally. But this is obvious, and platitudes irritate me. In reality my religion is probably only a form of psychological aberration with a tendency towards mysticism: there is a very particular psychological factor involved – my way of seeing the world, which is perhaps too respectful, too reverential, too childlike: I see everything in the world, objects as well as people and nature with a certain veneration, but this is to do with my character, not with my education and upbringing.

When did you learn to read and write? You've written about the importance of the spoken word: did you learn much before you could read – poetry or popular songs?

No, I began to write poetry at the same time as I began to write. But before I learnt to read and write I drew – that was when I was four. I only learnt to write when I was about seven, but unfortunately I lost my early poems. They were in a little notebook which I kept for years and then lost during the war. I illustrated the poems, because I wanted to paint and in fact did paint for a while. I've forgotten what was in these early poems, except for two words: one was *rosignolo* (nightingale) and the other was *verzura* (verdure), which are both extremely ornate literary words, as you can hear, so you can see I began in a really literary style. As for popular songs I only got interested in these much later, when I was about twenty-five or twenty-six.

What about Friulan: did you learn it as a child?

My relationship to Friulan is very curious because in fact it isn't my dialect at all, and it isn't even my mother's dialect. The Friulans are trilingual: first Friulan, which is their old language, which is a real language in its own light, not a dialect; second, Venetian, which was the language of the ruling class, brought in under Venetian rule; and, third, Italian. As my mother belonged in a way to the peasant élite of the area she spoke Venetian, not Friulan – as well as Italian, naturally. So I heard Friulan spoken by the peasants, who were absolutely authentic peasants; but I never spoke it myself, I only learnt it after I'd begun to write poetry in it. I learnt it as a sort of mystic act of love, a kind of *félibrisme*, like the Provençal poets. The first poems I wrote in Friulan were when I was about seventeen, and the reason behind this was very curious. As you know, at that time hermeticism was in vogue in Italy, which was a kind of provincial current of symbolism; Mallarmé was the principal influence and symbolism was widely taken up in Italy, mainly by Ungaretti (Rilke had some influence, too). The only person who followed the more important, more European poets like Eliot and Pound was Montale,[3] who represents a kind of marginal hermeticism.

The central idea of hermetic poetry was the idea of the language

Ungaretti; Rainer Maria Rilke in the Black Forest, 1913

of poetry as an absolute language. There is in fact a language of
poetry and a language of prose in every literary context, but the
hermetics unconsciously exaggerated this idea and thus adopted
for poetry a language for poetry, and took this to its extreme
limits: effectively this meant complete incomprehensibility, an
absence of communication. I took up Friulan as a special language
for poetry – i.e. the complete opposite of any tendency towards
realism. It was the maximum of irrealism, the maximum of
hermetic obscurity. However, once I came in contact with dialect
it inevitably had an effect, even though originally I only adopted
it for purely literary reasons: as soon as I took it up, I realized I
had touched on something living and real and it acted like a
boomerang. It was through Friulan that I came to understand
some of the real world of the peasantry. Of course, at first I under-
stood it imperfectly in an aesthetic way. I founded a small academy
of Friulan poetry, which produced some of the best young post-

war poets; but it was a mysticizing 'poeticizing' understanding somewhat like *Mistral* in Switzerland and the Provençal *félibres*. Yet once I'd taken this step I couldn't stop and so I started using dialect not as a hermetic-aestheticist device but more and more as an objective and realist element: this reached its culmination in my novels, where Roman dialect is used in a way which is the exact opposite of how I used Friulan at the beginning.

When you were at school did you feel the weight of fascism a great deal?

No, because I was born in a fascist age and a fascist world and I didn't notice fascism, just as a fish does not notice he is in the water. That was while I was a child. But when I was about fourteen or fifteen I gave up reading adventure stories and stopped saying my Hail Mary; I became an agnostic and started having literary ambitions; I began to read my first serious books, Dostoyevsky and Shakespeare. At the same time a gap emerged between me and the society, but my anti-fascism was absolutely cultural. As soon as I began to read real authors like Dostoyevsky and Shakespeare, and then people like Rimbaud and the hermetics, who belonged to a culture which fascism disapproved of and rejected, I felt myself outside society (or the society began to be challenged unconsciously by me). The thing which produced this was my reading these poets. As with the peasants and Friulan, it only needed a moment to make me realize I was on the side of the opposition. From the start, my opposition was an ingenuous one, it was purely in the realm of ideas; I just thought it was normal and easy to discuss things and when I spoke up on a literary topic in public meetings, in the GUFs[4] or in one of the pseudo-cultural meetings the fascists organized from time to time I did so ingenuously without realizing that this was an act of rebellion. Then gradually I realized and moved over to the side of the Resistance.

Moving round so much when you were young must have been fairly disconcerting: how old were you when you first really settled down and made friends with whom you could have regular discussions?

Francesco Leonetti; Roberto Roversi

Bologna was the first place where I had a real cultural milieu. I
went to *liceo* in Bologna and started university there. I made some
of my closest friends like Francesco Leonetti[5] and Roberto
Roversi[6] there. We founded the review *Officina*[7] there, and
these associations have lasted. I also met Roberto Longhi[8] in
Bologna, and I was supposed to do my thesis with him in the
history of art, but during the war I lost my thesis notes and had
to change. Anyway Bologna was where I made my first decisive
contacts.

Then there was the long stay in Friuli during the war, where we
were evacuated to avoid the bombing in Bologna (where my
brother was killed fighting with the partisans). Friuli was the
second main milieu, although it was somewhat artificial, as I'd
chosen it as a kind of ideal site for poetry and my aestheticizing,
mystic fantasies. However, it was important for me and in particular it was there that I became a marxist, in a rather unusual way.

As I told you, I discovered the Friulan peasants objectively through the utterly subjective use of their dialect. In the immediate post-war period the *braccianti* (day-labourers) were engaged in a massive struggle against the big landlords in Friuli. For the first time in my life I found myself physically absolutely unprepared because my anti-fascism was purely aesthetic and cultural, it was not political. For the first time I found myself faced with the class struggle, and I had no hesitation: I sided with the *braccianti* at once. The *braccianti* had red scarves round their necks and from that moment I embraced communism, just like that, emotionally. Then I read Marx and some of the marxists. So Friuli was very important for me. But the place I've worked in longest is Rome: I came here in 1950 and have lived here ever since.

What were you doing your thesis with Longhi on? And how did you lose it?

I was supposed to do it on contemporary Italian painting: I'd done brief chapters on Carrà, De Pisis and Morandi. What happened was that I took the text with me when I was called up in 1943. I was only in the army a week when the Armistice[9] was announced (8 September). I lost my thesis because it was in the barracks when we were taken prisoner – two Germans in a tank took our whole regiment prisoner. I and a friend who were the least military people in the outfit unwittingly performed our first act of resistance: instead of surrendering our arms to the Germans we threw them into a ditch, and then during a burst of machine-gun fire we jumped into a ditch and waited for the regiment to go off and then escaped. It was a completely instinctive and involuntary beginning to my resistance.

How was it that you decided then to do your degree on Pascoli?

I chose Pascoli[10] because he was a poet who was very close to some of my own interests at the time, and very close to the world of Friulan peasants. Pascoli's characters and his settings, his children,

University thesis: Italian painting (*hommage* to Morandi – Stella with bottles in *Accattone*)

the birds and all that, his magical and *highly* artificial world, which is falsely ingenuous – all this was very close to my taste. Besides, it wasn't a time when you could do a degree on a more modern poet, so it was a choice of the lesser evil. I couldn't say I was enormously interested in Pascoli, but I was interested all the same. Moreover, Pascoli is basically the forerunner of Montale[11] on one side, and of the *crepuscolari* (twilight poets)[12] on the other: he's an important branch of Italian literature. Five or six years ago Pascoli's sister published a biography of him which shows him to have been such a monster morally and psychologically that it is no wonder that he has played such a major role in Italian poetry.

To come back to marxism: from what you've said it sounds as though you came to it initially through supporting the Communist Party, rather than vice versa, which is perhaps strange for an intellectual.

University thesis: Giovanni Pascoli; 'About Stalin I knew nothing'

How did this happen? Did you actually join the PCI? And roughly when and how did you study marxism as a science?

Yes, in a way you're right to say that I supported first communism and then marxism, but it should really be changed to say that I first supported communists and then marxism. You must remember that Italy was and still is in a fairly unusual position in western Europe. While the peasant world has completely disappeared in the major industrialized countries like France and England (you can't talk about the peasantry in the classic sense of the word there) in Italy it still survives, although there has been a decline in recent years. In the immediate post-war period the peasantry still lived in a completely peasant world just like it was one or two centuries ago. My mother used to have to go to bed by candle-light. My relationship with the peasantry is very direct, as it is in most Italians – almost all of us have at least one peasant grandfather, in the classical sense. Now these communists in Friuli were peasants, and this is very important. Perhaps if they'd been urban working-class communists the class factor would have been too strong for me and I would have resisted; but I couldn't hold out against peasant communists, who are the ones who make revolutions, in Russia, in Cuba, in Algeria – although they make them in a pre-class way (which is a rather unorthodox thing for a communist to say): this is perhaps why there is such a strangely ambiguous symbiosis, which is also a valid one, as well as being poetic, between the peasantry of the third world and the students here. That's the main point: once my support for these peasant communists was established all the rest was easy. I gradually read the texts and became a marxist. But you must remember that everybody in Italy is a marxist, just as everybody in Italy is a Catholic. An intelligent priest will always analyse society in marxist terms, even the Pope does this. A phrase used by Paul VI which I put into *Uccellacci e Uccellini* was taken by everybody to be a phrase of Marx's. Marxism is part of Italian culture. I did join the party for about a year in the period 1947–48, but when my membership card lapsed I didn't bother to renew it.

You once[13] said that there was some hope for marxist criticism within Italian culture during the period when the Politecnico *was first published, then came Stalinism and then a period of renewed hope with the introduction of Lukács and other unorthodox marxist writers. What was your relationship with the* Politecnico? *And how would you characterize Stalinism – from your comment it sounds as though you don't date it from the immediate post-war period?*

I didn't have any relationship with the *Politecnico* because I was at Casarsa at the time, out in a backwater, whereas the *Politecnico* was in Milan and Florence: I only lived it as an indirect experience.

It's a commonplace to say that there were great hopes for communism in that period in Italy, everybody said it, and it's a bit embarrassing to repeat it. Stalinism, however, had a particular kind of character in Italy: it was indistinguishable from the policies of Togliatti. I don't want to accuse Togliatti of participating in Stalin's crimes – I suspend judgment on this; it's a question for the historians – I only hope that it will be marxist historians who deal with it, and if there's anything grave to be said that it will be said by them. But Stalinism in Italy took the form of Togliatti's policies, which were tacticist, diplomatic, authoritarian and paternalistic. The PCI leadership always had a paternalist attitude towards the rank and file, never going to the bottom of problems, wheeling and dealing with the political enemy (like over the Concordat). I have always been against Togliatti's policy. About Stalin I knew nothing: instinctively I thought that what I heard against him was just calumny, so my anti-Stalinism is a bit odd – it came from my critical attitude towards the Togliattian policy of the Communist Party.

Could you say something about Gramsci, particularly as you've been, let's say, 'accused'[14] *of being a Gramscian? When did you first read him, and was he an important influence on you?*

When I spoke earlier about reading marxist texts, the most important, even more important than Marx himself, was Gramsci. Marx, naturally, was rather difficult when I first read him, and besides he was rather distant from me for various reasons. Whereas Gramsci's ideas coincided with mine; they won me over immediately, and he had a fundamental role in my formation. I first read him in the period 1948–49.

Do you think you can call Gramsci a populist – and what sense would it have for you to do so?

No, I don't think you can. Though I'd like to say first that I don't give any pejorative meaning to the word 'populist'. It is marxist moralists who use it (along with the word 'humanitarian') to condemn other kinds of marxists. I don't agree with this at all. For me populism and humanitarianism are two real facts of history: all marxist intellectuals come from bourgeois backgrounds; the initial impetus to become marxists can only be of a populist or a humanitarian kind, and so this factor is perforce in all bourgeois marxists, including Gramsci. But I don't find this a negative factor, it is simply part of the unavoidable transition from the bourgeois class in which one is born and moulded to the adoption of a different ideology, the ideology of another social class.

You said somewhere[15] that 'apart from the major cities in Italy, all the rest of the country, which is all one huge province, is permeated by the Catholicism of the Counter-Reformation'. Yet you seem to place your hopes precisely in the very part of Italy which you say has been most subjected to the Counter-Reformation – rural Italy. How do you reach this paradoxical conclusion?

I'm a bit surprised by the question, because I don't think I ever said anything quite like that, that I expected much from the Italy of Counter-Reformation Catholicism. Or, if I said it, I said it ironically. But I want to accept that I did say it, because now that you bring it up I realize I could have said it. For the following reasons: the Protestant movement in northern Europe was the first bourgeois revolution. Luther was the first great hero of the bourgeoisie. In Italy this first bourgeois revolution never took place. Whereas in northern Europe Protestantism was the religion of the new bourgeoisie, in Italy the bourgeoisie did not emerge like this and carry through its first revolution: the Italian bourgeoisie was born through inertia, let's say, through imitating the European bourgeoisies, passively. But then it didn't have a second, liberal revolution, either. So a bourgeoisie was formed which was wildly in contradiction with the country's traditions – a bourgeoisie must be Protestant and liberal, yet in Italy it emerged in a Counter-Reformation world, a world of peasants. So there are profound contradictions here. In fact, the Italian bourgeoisie is extremely strange, because it is simultaneously lay and Catholic, liberal and Counter-Reformation, i.e. it is nothing. *Qualunquismo*[16] is basically the result of these contradictions, together with the degeneration of humanism, which is its main ingredient.

Now at this point in history the peasantry is waking up every-where. It is the peasants who have made revolutions, who have become the protagonists of one of the greatest events of con-temporary history – the emergence of the third world. The Italian peasantry, too, is becoming revolutionary. The new left in Italy is, oddly enough, emerging on the most peasant and Catholic terrain – terrain which at first sight might seem the most conservative. Don Milani[17] is the most obvious example of a kind of new left which comes near to the Cultural Revolution in China; Don Milani came from the depths of the backwoods, high up in the Apennines. So, even if I never actually said it before, I'm prepared to say it now: yes, it is from the Counter-Reformation world of the Italian peasantry that the most left-wing impetus comes today.

So you ought to feel optimistic politically.

Optimistic about some tiny minorities of Catholics from peasant backgrounds, who may produce a few pleasant surprises, like Don Milani. But, objectively, what is happening is that the North is colonizing the South and transforming the peasants into petits bourgeois, turning them into consumers. Italy as a whole is moving towards a consumer civilization, it's turning into a horrible petit bourgeois world, so my flash of optimism is buried under the most profound pessimism.

But surely the fact that the bourgeoisie has never managed to impose itself in Italy as a hegemonic class, that it is such a nullity, as you put it, must leave more room for successful contestation? I still don't quite understand your political attitude towards the various classes in Italy, which is important because your writings and films have a strong class content. What is your political sociology of Italian classes?

That is an impossible question, particularly in my case. I partly answered the question when I was talking about the Friulan *braccianti* and when I said that I belonged to the typical Italian petit bourgeoisie. Sociologically, my position is not very typical;

in fact it is not even definable. There is an emotional basis which probably comes from my early childhood and the clash with my father and the whole petit bourgeois environment. My hatred for the bourgeoisie is not documentable or arguable. It's just there and that's it. But it's not a moralistic condemnation; it is total and unmitigated, but it is based on passion, not on moralism. Moralism is a typical disease of part of the Italian left, which has imported typical bourgeois moralistic attitudes into marxist, or at any rate communist, ideology.

As for the other popular class – the working class – I've had a very difficult relationship with them, which was initially romantic, populist and humanitarian. When you are born in a petit bourgeois milieu, you think the whole world is the same as the environment you live in. As soon as I got to see another kind of world, naturally my own was thrown into crisis. When I realized that Friulan *braccianti* existed, and that their psychology, their education, their mentality, their soul, their sexuality were all different, my world broke down; I could no longer love the bourgeois élite and hate the bourgeoisie; a new feeling emerged, the feeling of taking part from outside, though this was made authentic and validated by the real love I felt for the workers, and especially for the peasants.

I've never had a close acquaintance with the working class because in the towns I lived in as a child I only knew the people who were at school with me, who all came from bourgeois families. Then I was at Casarsa, where I met peasants, but no workers. From there I came straight to Rome, which is not a working-class town. Eighteen years ago when I first came here there was no industry at all. Now there is the odd small factory on the Via Tiburtina. But basically Rome is a bureaucratic, administrative and tourist town, almost a colonial town. What I did have here, which was an extremely traumatic and a sociologically very vital experience, was contact with the Roman subproletariat. For the first time I threw myself into a socially completely different world which forced me to be objective towards it. I had to make a marxist diagnosis of it. Although the Friulan *braccianti* were poorer than I was economically and intellectually, basically they still belonged to the same world as I did, because the petit bourgeoisie has its roots in the peasantry. The relationship between a Friulan *bracciante* and me was almost one of brother to brother; there was no gap between my mother and a Friulan *bracciante*. But with the Roman subproletariat I was confronted with a completely different world. On the one hand I was traumatized, just like an English person might be traumatized coming to Italy, because it was something completely unexpected; and on the other hand, it forced me into an objective diagnosis. So, whereas at first I used dialect for subjective reasons, as a purely poetic language, on the contrary when I came down to Rome I began to use the dialect of the Roman subproletariat in an objective way, to get the most exact possible description of the world I was faced with.

This is only one of the many literary shifts you've made in your career. You once[18] said that 'a literary training jeopardizes one's entire existence as a writer'. What did you mean?

You're like one of the Furies, reminding me of things I've forgotten. I think what I meant was simply that the first poetry one reads is unforgettable. *Macbeth* and Dostoyevsky's *Idiot* I still remember with emotion, they are an important factor in my life, like Rimbaud. I meant more than something cultural, I meant something existential within culture. Sometimes culture can produce feelings so strong that they are like the feelings produced by nature, and these feelings then go to form one's psychology; when it is formed, it is hard to change: it may perhaps evolve, but something basically fixed remains. I think that's all I meant.

Two critics who have written about your poetry have pronounced apparently opposing judgments: Franco Fortini[19] has said that you have 'brought all the powers of expression of modern poetry to bear on an ideological content which can be taken for granted'; Alberto Asor Rosa[20] has said that your 'formula is a new ideology plus traditional forms'. Why do you think they were able to come up with such contradictory opinions?

Both seem wrong . . . and right. Both are justifiable. I am not an inventor of ideologies. I am not a thinker and have never aspired to be. Sometimes, within the context of an ideology I have an intuition and thus have sometimes anticipated the professional ideologues. And stylistically I am a *pasticheur*: I use the most disparate stylistic material – dialect poetry, decadent poetry, certain attempts at socialist poetry; there is always a stylistic contamination in my writings, I don't have a completely invented personal style of my own, though my style is recognizable. If you read a page of mine you can recognize it's mine fairly easily. I am not recognizable as an inventor of a stylistic formula, but for the degree of intensity to which I bring the contamination and mixture of the various styles. Neither is right, because what counts is the degree of violence and intensity – and this involves both the form and the styles, as well as the ideology. What counts is the depth of feeling, the passion I put into things; it isn't so much the novelty of the content, nor the novelty of form.

The question of what you call 'contamination'[21] is partly connected with the specific problems of Italian as a language. Could you tell me how your thinking about Italian as a medium has evolved as you have moved from poetry to novels and on to the cinema?

First, I'd like to say that you can see my *pasticheur* nature in the cinema, as in the other forms (*pasticheur* by passion, that is, not by calculation). If you see a bit of one of my films, you can tell it's mine from the tone. It's not like with, say, Godard or Chaplin who have invented a style which is completely their own. Mine is made up of various styles. You can always feel underneath my love for Dreyer, Mizoguchi and Chaplin – and some of Tati, etc., etc. Basically, my nature hasn't changed in the move from literature to cinema.

My ideas on the relationship between the Italian language and the cinema are much better expressed in my essays on the subject, but very simply let me say this: at first I thought the shift from literature to cinema involved simply a change of technique, as I have often changed techniques. Then gradually, as I worked in the cinema and got more and more into it I came to understand that the cinema is not a literary technique; it is a language of its own. The first idea that came to me was that I had instinctively given up writing novels and then gradually given up poetry, too, as a protest against Italy and Italian society. I have several times said I would like to change nationality, give up Italian and take up another language; so I came to the idea that the language of the cinema is not a national language, it is a language I like to define as 'transnational' (not 'international' because this is ambiguous) and 'transclass' – i.e. a worker or a bourgeois, a Ghanaian or an American, when they use the language of the cinema all use a common system of signs. So at first I thought it was a protest against my society. Then gradually I realized it was even more complicated than that: the passion that had taken the form of a great love for literature and for life gradually stripped itself of the love for literature and turned to what it really was – a passion for life, for reality, for physical, sexual, objectual [*oggettuale*], existential reality around me. This is my first and only great love and the cinema in a way forced me to turn to it and express only it.

How did this come about? By studying the cinema as a system of signs, I came to the conclusion that it is a non-conventional and non-symbolic language [*linguaggio*] unlike the written or spoken language [*lingua*], and expresses reality not through symbols but via reality itself. If I have to express you, I express you through yourself; if I want to express that tree I express it through itself. The cinema is a language [*linguaggio*] which expresses reality with reality. So the question is: what is the difference between the cinema and reality? Practically none. I realized that the cinema is a system of signs whose semiology corresponds to a possible semiology of the system of signs of reality itself. So the cinema forced me to remain always at the level of reality, right inside reality: when I make a film I am always in reality, among the trees and among people like yourself; there is no symbolic or conventional filter between me and reality, as there is in literature. So in practice the cinema was an explosion of my love for reality.

I'd like to go right back and ask you how you started out in the cinema. You've said that you thought about making movies when you were a child, and then gave up the idea. What was the first film you saw – and did it make a strong impression?

Unfortunately, I can't remember the first film I saw because I was too young. But I can tell you about my first relationship with the cinema, as I remember it, when I was five years old – which was a bit weird, and certainly had an erotic-sexual facet to it. I remember that I was looking at a publicity folder for a film showing a tiger tearing a man to pieces. Obviously the tiger was on top of the man but for some unknown reason it seemed to me with my child's imagination that the tiger had half swallowed the man and the other half was still protruding out of its jaws. I terribly wanted to see the film; naturally my parents wouldn't take me, which I bitterly regret to this day. So this image of the tiger eating the man, which is a masochistic and perhaps cannibalistic image, is the first thing that has remained impressed on me – though obviously I saw other movies at the time, but I can't remember them.

Then what I was about seven or eight, when I was living at Sacile, I used to go to a cinema run by some priests, and I can remember bits of some of the silent movies I saw there, and I can remember the transition to the talkies: the first talkie I saw was a war movie.

So much for my cinema pre-history. Then when I was in Bologna I joined a film club and saw some of the classics – all of René Clair, the first Renoirs, some Chaplin, and so on. That's where my great love for the cinema started. I remember going in for a competition in the local GUF and writing a mad D'Annunzian piece, completely barbaric and sensual. Then the war interrupted everything. After the war came neo-realism. I can remember going specially from Casarsa to Udine to see *Bicycle Thieves*, and above all *Rome, Open City*, which I saw up in Friuli, which was a real trauma that I still remember with emotion. But these films were only remote cultural objects for me while I was still living in the provinces, like the books and reviews I used to get sent to me. Then I came down to Rome, not thinking at all about going into the cinema, and when I wrote my first novel, *Ragazzi di Vita*, some directors asked me to do scripts for them. The first was Mario Soldati, an early Sophia Loren called *La Donna del Fiume*, which I did with Giorgio Bassani.[22] Then there was *Le Notti di Cabiria* with Fellini, and then quite a lot of others, and so the desire to make films naturally came back.

You seem to have worked with directors with whom you have little in common, people like Bolognini, for example. You don't seem to me to have much in common with Fellini either. The person with whom you do share a great deal is obviously Rossellini, yet you never worked with him. Why is this?

Purely practical reasons. When I came to Rome I was completely broke. I didn't have a job, and I spent a year in extreme poverty – some days I didn't even have the money to go to the barber, for example, so you can see I was in the direst poverty. Then I started teaching at a school at Ciampino, so I went to live at Ponte Mammolo, which is a slum right out on the outskirts of Rome. I had to do a terribly long journey, and I only earned 27,000 lire (just over £16 at the time) a month. When my first novel came out I started to get a few royalties, but I still needed a job badly, so I became a script-writer. Obviously I couldn't choose who I was going to work with, it was the other way round. But I was very lucky, I always had good people to work with. Although this was all commissioned work, I feel that some of the scripts (like *La Notte Brava*) are among the best literary works I have ever done: I've collected some of them together in *Alì Dagli Occhi Azzurri*.

What part did you have in Le Notti di Cabiria?

I wrote all the low life parts. As there were these kind of characters in *Ragazzi di Vita* Fellini thought I knew that world, as indeed I did because I had lived out at Ponte Mammolo, where lots of pimps and petty thieves and whores live; all the setting, and

Cabiria's relations with the other whores and especially the episode about Divine Love are all done by me – the story's in *Alì Dagli Occhi Azzurri*. My main contribution was in the dialogue, which has been a bit lost because Fellini's use of dialect is fairly different from mine. Basically, the first draft of the dialogue and at least half the episode are mine.

You've worked quite a lot with Bassani: how did you meet?

We're very close friends and we've worked together a lot. I first met him when he was running the review *Botteghe Oscure*. I went to see him professionally, and then we became great friends. I wrote for his review, and we both admire each other's work.

Apart from the period when you were doing scripts for other directors, there is nothing to ask you about your collaborators, as you seem to be the complete auteur *of all your own films. Did you feel very disappointed with what other directors did to your texts?*

No, a director has the right to make these changes. But if I wanted to describe certain milieus, certain faces and gestures which were transformed from how I'd imagined them, then naturally, there was a gulf I wanted to bridge – apart from my long-standing desire to make movies. As for my own films, I never conceived of making a film which would be the work of a group. I've always thought of a film as the work of an author, not only the script and the direction, but the choice of sets and locations, the characters, even the clothes, I choose everything – not to mention the music. I have collaborators, like Danilo Donati, my costume designer; I have the first idea, but I wouldn't know how to make the thing, and so he does all that, extremely well, with excellent taste and zest.

NOTES

1. Pasolini started again in the summer of 1968 – to denounce the student movement. See 'Il PCI ai giovani!!', *Nuovi Argomenti* 10 (nuova serie). For some of the reactions to Pasolini's text see *Nuovi Argomenti*, and *L'Espresso*, 16 June 1968.

2. Though in *Prisma* 3/4 Gian Paolo Prandstraller has a photograph of Pasolini entitled 'Pier Paolo's Confirmation photograph', which is credited to the author's private album.

3. 'And Montale, as you perhaps know, is Italy's major poet (though I think the greatest living Italian poet is Penna, who is completely uninfluenced by anybody, except perhaps by the Alexandrians). Montale was greatly influenced by Pound and through Montale Pound has influenced a whole generation of young poets, not to mention the most recent *avant-garde* – Sanguineti, for example, effectively has done nothing but regurgitate Pound, somewhat Italianized. Anyway, Montale represents a kind of marginal hermeticism.'

4. Fascist University Youth.

5. Francesco Leonetti figures in several of Pasolini's films: as Herod II in *The Gospel According to St Matthew*, as the voice of the crow in *Uccellacci e Uccellini*, as the Servant of Laius whom Oedipus visits in *Oedipus Rex* and as the puppet-master in *Che Cosa Sono le Nuvole?* He is a playwright, and currently editor of the *avant-garde* review *Che Fare?*

6. Roberto Roversi, poet, critic and editor of *Rendiconti*, produced, like *Officina*, from his bookshop in Bologna.

7. *Officina*: a review published in the mid fifties from Bologna. Most of Pasolini's work in it has been reprinted in the volume *Passione e Ideologia*, Milan, 1960.

8. Roberto Longhi: famous art critic and historian; specialist on Venetian painting and the Ferrara School; editor of the cultural review *Paragone*. Pasolini dedicated *Mamma Roma* to Longhi *'cui sono debitore della mia folgorazione figurativa'*.

9. The Armistice was between Italy and the Allies: it meant, of course, that the military lull was over and that Italy was now at war with Germany. Cf. the Puccini film which Pasolini worked on, *Il Carro Armato dell'8 Settembre*.

10. Giovanni Pascoli (1855–1912). Pasolini's text on him is in *Officina*, May 1955, and now, slightly modified, in *Passione e Ideologia*. There is a famous text on Pascoli by Croce in *La Letteratura della Nuova Italia*, Bari, 1954.

11. Eugenio Montale was born in Genoa in 1896. After the Second World War he was for a time editor of the conservative Milan daily, *Il Corriere della Sera*. He is a prestigious critic and translator as well as poet.

12. The *crepuscolari* were the first (poetic) opponents of D'Annunzio. The two chief exponents of the trend (whose name was bestowed on them by G. A. Borgese) were Guido Gozzano and Sergio Corazzini.

Their poetry, although more adventurous than D'Annunzio's, was almost all about death.

13. In answer to '8 Domande sulla Critica Litteraria in Italia', *Nuovi Argomenti*, 44–5. This is one of Pasolini's more enlightening texts on the whole role of marxism and of Gramsci in particular in Italian literature and criticism. The *Politecnico* was the review founded by Elio Vittorini immediately after the end of the war. It pursued a resolutely marxist policy independent of any one political group, and eventually collapsed at the end of 1947, having already had to change from a weekly to a monthly. It lived under intense pressure from the PCI, exemplified in the exchange of letters between Vittorini and Togliatti. It remains an *avant-garde* political experience in marxist culture. For a summing up, see Franco Fortini, *Che cosa è stato 'Il Politecnico'*, now in Franco Fortini, *Dieci Inverni*, Milan, 1957.

14. In particular by Alberto Asor Rosa in *Scrittori e Popolo*, Rome, 1965.

15. In answer in *Nuovi Argomenti*, 44–5.

16. '*Qualunquismo* is the practicist-empiricist degeneration of Italian humanism' (Alberto Moravia). It was also the name given to a far right-wing political movement in the immediate post-war period.

17. 'Don Milani was a priest who died two years ago of cancer. He lived at Barbiana and set up a small school there for the children who lived in the area, miles from anywhere, up in the mountains between Bologna and Florence. He wrote a book about his experiences at Barbiana, and then later on a group of his pupils also wrote a book entitled *Lettera ad una Professoressa* [*Letter to a Schoolmistress*], which I urge you to read and you will see how these peasants born in the depths of the backwoods, even more profoundly backward than the South – where at least there is banditry and some kind of revolutionary tradition – have begun to show characteristics which are typical of part of the American new left and of the Red Guards in China.'

18. In 'La Posizione', *Officina* 1, 1956.

19. Franco Fortini, *Le Poesie Italiane di Questi Anni, Il Menabò* 2 (1960): a brilliant over-view of Italian poetry in the late fifties. Fortini is a remarkable poet, critic and essayist, who has consistently played an important role right from the time of *Il Politecnico* through *Officina* and *Ragionamenti* and on to *Quaderni Rossi* and *Quaderni Piacentini*. Pasolini acknowledges his debt in *Uccellacci e Uccellini*, p. 59.

20. Alberto Asor Rosa, *op. cit.*

21. For a fuller statement of 'contamination', see the text of Pasolini's discussion at the Centro Sperimentale [Film School] in *Bianco e*

Nero 6 (1964). There is a truncated version of this in English in *Film Quarterly*, vol. 18, no. 4 (summer 1965).

22. Giorgio Bassani was born in Bologna in 1916 of a Ferrara family. As well as editing *Botteghe Oscure*, he also edited *Paragone* for a time. Author of a series of stories about Ferrara and several novels, including *Il Giardino dei Finzi-Contini*. He has worked with Pasolini on numerous films, including one based on his own story, *Una Notte del '43*. He dubbed Orson Welles in *La Ricotta*.

Franco Citti: *Accattone; Mamma Roma*

2: Accattone

Had Accattone *been going round in your mind for a long time before you made it as a film – was it conceived as a cinematic subject?*

The idea of making a film and the idea of doing *Accattone* came together. Before that I'd written another thing for the cinema, *La Commare Secca*; but this project got blocked, and so I replaced it with *Accattone*, which seemed a better idea.

What do you mean 'it got blocked'? It didn't get financial backing?

No, I was supposed to do *La Commare Secca*, but then I changed my mind and wrote *Accattone*. Then *Accattone* ran into trouble (which I talk about in the preface to the book of *Accattone*), but *La Commare Secca* would probably have run into the same difficulty. I decided to replace *La Commare Secca* with *Accattone*.

Previously when you talked about the shift from writing to making a movie, you said the only big change was the lack of metaphor in the cinema.[1] Do you still think this is the biggest problem?

Well, I said that a bit carelessly. I didn't know very much about the cinema, and it was a long time before I started all my linguistic research on the cinema. It was just a casual remark, but was intuitively fairly prophetic: Jakobson, followed by Barthes, has spoken of the cinema as a metonymic, as opposed to a metaphoric art. Metaphor is an essentially linguistic and literary figure of speech which is difficult to render in the cinema except in extremely rare cases – for example, if I wanted to represent happiness I could do it with birds flying in the sky. It wasn't that I felt the difficulty of not being able to use metaphor, I was glad not to have to use it, because as I have said, the cinema represents reality with reality; it is metonymic and not metaphoric. Reality doesn't need metaphors to express itself. If I want to express you I express you through yourself, I couldn't use metaphors to express you. In the cinema it is as though reality expressed itself with itself, without metaphors, and without anything insipid and conventional and symbolic.

That comes through particularly in your treatment of Franco Citti in the first film. How did you find him?

He was the brother of my oldest friend in Rome, Sergio Citti. I met Sergio Citti about a year after I got here in 1950 and we became great friends. He helped me enormously in all my novels, he was like a living dictionary for me. I used to jot down notes at home and then I would go over and see him to get him to check the jokes and the local slang of the Roman characters, in which he was extremely proficient. I'd known his brother Franco for years, ever since he was a small boy, and when I had to choose the people for *Accattone* I thought of him for the part immediately.

You have said that the fact that you made Accattone *during the Tambroni government[2] influenced the way you ended the film – what did you mean?*

The Tambroni government did not influence the film. I knew and cared nothing about Tambroni, who was a complete nonentity and could therefore not possibly have the slightest influence on me. What I meant was that *Accattone* was a film that could emerge in Italy at a certain cultural moment – i.e. when neo-realism was dead. Neo-realism was the expression in the cinema of the Resistance, of the rediscovery of Italy, with all our hopes for a new kind of society. This lasted until the late fifties. After that neo-realism died because Italy changed: the establishment reconsolidated its position on petit bourgeois and clerical bases. So I said that *Accattone* is what it is (apart from the fact that it is what it is because I am made the way I am) for external cultural reasons – by which I meant not just the Tambroni episode, but the whole re-establishment of officialdom and hypocrisy. The Italian bourgeoisie had closed one cultural period, the age of neo-realism.

You changed Citti's voice, didn't you?

Yes, I had him dubbed, but it was a mistake. At the time I was a bit unsure of myself. Later I had him dub himself and he was excellent – and I even got him to dub other Roman characters. Anyway it was, let's say, a theoretical error. Paolo Ferraro who dubbed him in *Accattone* was extremely good and I think he added something to the character because dubbing, while altering a character, also makes it more mysterious; it enlarges and enriches it. I'm against filming in sync. There was a seminar at Amalfi recently, organized by *Filmcritica*, which came out with a declaration in favour of sync. sound, which I see I've unwittingly signed, but in fact I'm against it because I think that dubbing enriches a character; it is part of my taste for pastiche; it raises a character out of the zone of naturalism. I believe deeply in reality, in realism, but I can't stand naturalism.

So you're not only for dubbing later, you also like having an actor dubbed by another person's voice?

Unfortunately, it's rather difficult in Italy because of the dubbers. They're not quite as awful as they are in France, where they really are execrable, but all the same they are extremely conformist. What I often do is to 'cross' two non-professionals. I believe in polyvalence in a character. I like elaborating a character. The main point is that my love for reality is philosophical and reverential, but it is not naturalistic.

But actors depend for their identity on a number of factors, among which their voice can be crucial – Robert Mitchum or John Wayne could not exist without their voices.

That is true, but I'm not interested in actors. The only time I'm interested in an actor is when I use an actor to act an actor. For example, I never use extras in my films, because they are just hacks. Their faces are brutalized by living all their life at Cinecittà, surrounded by whores who are always hanging around there. When I shot *The Gospel* I went round and chose all the extras myself one by one from among the peasants and the people in the villages round where we were shooting. But when I made *La Ricotta*, where the characters are real extras, I used real extras. I'm only interested in an actor when he's acting an actor, I'm not interested in him *qua* actor. The fact that an actor may depend on his voice is something that interests me very little.

Do you mind what happens to your films when they go abroad? For example in Spain Christ was dubbed with a voice which completely changed his character. In the Italian version you gave Christ a rather hard voice which none of the foreign dubbings reproduced.

Far worse things than that happen in Spain. In a country where people are still garrotted I can resign myself to the idea that my characters may be badly dubbed. All I can say is that I despise anybody who is responsible for doing things like that. Part of the dubbing in Spain I organized myself, but it was half done when I got there and it was horrible, so I tried to fix the other half as best I could. In civilized countries like England and America it came out with sub-titles, which I prefer.

When you mentioned neo-realism you defined it as the expression of the Resistance. I'd like you to expand on this, because I have just seen

Extras: chosen faces for *The Gospel*, and 'real' extras for *La Ricotta* (being entertained with a striptease at lunchtime)

two of the films Rossellini made during the fascist period, La Nave
Bianca *and* L'Uomo della Croce: *stylistically, these are exactly the
same as the films he made during the so-called 'neo-realist period'.
Have you seen these films, and can you see any change in Rossellini's
style between the fascist period and the post-war period?*

I agree I did say that neo-realism is a product of the Resistance,
and I stand by that remark. But, having said that, I must add that
neo-realism is still full of elements from the preceding period. I
have often criticized neo-realism – for example in *Officina*. I
remember criticizing neo-realism for not having sufficient intellectual strength to transcend the culture which preceded it. I
criticized it for being naturalistic, above all. Naturalism was a
taste which went right back to the nineteenth century, to Verga,
for example. I also criticized it for being *crepuscolare*,[3] which is
another characteristic of Italian poetry, exemplified by Gozzano,
for example – I don't know if there's anything like it in England;
in France there are people like Laforgue, a sector of the deca-
dents. Then I also criticized it for remaining subjective and
lyricizing, which was another feature of the cultural epoch
before the Resistance. So, neo-realism is a cultural product of
the Resistance as regards content and message but stylistically
it is still tied to pre-Resistance culture. Basically there is something rather hybrid about it. Anyway, if you think about other
products of the European Resistance, much of the poetry is
written in the same style as before the war, using surrealism, for
example. It's a phenomenon common to the whole of Europe, I
think.

As for Rossellini, no I haven't seen those two films. When they
first came out I never had a chance to see them and now I'm not
too keen to see them – it's a bit because I've been too busy to see
them, and at bottom I just don't want to see them.

To go back to Accattone, *could you say something about the way you
were influenced in this by the three directors you have singled out:
Dreyer, Mizoguchi and Chaplin?*

Verga; Guido Gozzano

Well, I don't know if you can really talk about direct *influences*. I don't know if I was thinking about these authors when I was shooting the film, they are source references I made somewhat from the outside after I'd finished the film. When I was making it the only author I thought of directly was Masaccio. When I'd finished it I realized that some of my great loves had played a part in it. Why these three? Because they are all in their own way epic directors – not epic in the Brechtian sense of the word; I mean epic in the more mythic sense of the word – a more natural epicness which pertains more to things, to facts, to characters, to the story, without Brecht's detachment. I feel this mythic epicness in both Dreyer and Mizoguchi and Chaplin: all three see things from a point of view which is absolute, essential and in a certain way holy, reverential [*sacrale*].

Have you ever thought much about the question of producing a

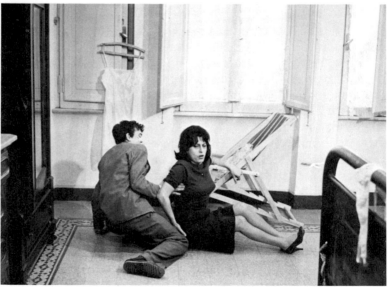

From the world of the subproletariat (Franco Citti in *Accattone*) to that of the petit bourgeoisie (Ettore Garofolo and Anna Magnani after falling down dancing to an old dance-tune in *Mamma Roma*)

Accattone: the dream — epic–mythic–fantastic?; *Mamma Roma:* petit-bourgeois ideals like going to Mass on Sunday, when the mother (Anna Magnani) tells her son (Ettore Garofolo) which particular member of the congregation might get him a job

*religious film within a Protestant culture as compared with a Catholic
culture? I think some of the French critics, Leenhardt in particular,
have written about this, with reference to Dreyer and Protestantism.*

No, I haven't studied this particularly because it is a problem
which can't arise in Italy: there is no objective relationship
between Catholicism and Protestantism in Italy, it's a purely
abstract problem. It might be a real problem in England or
Belgium, or even in France, but it's a problem you can't even
think about in Italy.

When you talked about the change from Accattone *to* Mamma Roma
in another interview[4] you said that the Anna Magnani character in
Mamma Roma *had petit bourgeois ideals, whereas the characters in*
Accattone *were not even aware of the existence of petit bourgeois
ideals and morality. But Accattone's dream about his own death
seems to me to be conceived very much along petit bourgeois lines, at
least along the lines of petit bourgeois religion.*

I'm rather surprised you should say that, because I've never
thought about it like that. It seems to me that Accattone's dream
has the characteristics I mentioned earlier, it is epic-mythic-
fantastic; these aren't typical characteristics of the petit bourgeoisie.
Perhaps you are referring to the salvation of the soul, but this isn't
a bourgeois problem because the bourgeoisie hasn't got a transcendental religion, except verbally; it's only catechistic and
liturgical, it isn't real. The bourgeoisie has replaced the problem
of the soul, which is transcendental, with conscience which is a
purely social and mundane thing. Accattone's metaphysical
projection of his own life into a world beyond is mythic and
popular; it isn't petit bourgeois, it's *pre*-bourgeois. The petit
bourgeois ideals I talked about in *Mamma Roma* were all petty
mundane ideals like a home, a job, keeping up appearances, the
radio, going to Mass on Sunday, whereas in *Accattone* I don't
think there's anything petit bourgeois like that. The Catholicism
in *Accattone* still retains the pre-bourgeois, pre-industrial and

Accattone: setting up the end; Accattone's two friends get busted

therefore mythical features which are typical only of the people –
in fact the final sign of the Cross is done wrong; perhaps you didn't
notice this, but instead of touching their left shoulder and then the
right, they do the right shoulder first and then the left, just like the
children who cross themselves while the funeral is going past, who
make the same mistake: the sign they make is not even a Christian
sign, it's just vaguely religious and protective, but it isn't Catholic
in the orthodox – and therefore bourgeois – sense of the word.

NOTES

1. Metaphor: see interview in *Filmcritica* 116 (January 1962). Cf. *Film Culture* 24 (spring 1962).
2. Tambroni government: Tambroni was a Christian Democrat who led a government which depended on right-wing, including monarchist and fascist, support. It was brought down in the summer of 1960 by popular demonstrations.
3. *Crepuscolare:* see note 12 in previous chapter.
4. *Filmcritica* 125 (September 1962).

3: Mamma Roma

I'd like to go on to Mamma Roma *now and ask you about this conflict in the Anna Magnani character: the fact that she has petit bourgeois ideals but in fact can't realize them – the futility of petit bourgeois morality. And why did you choose Anna Magnani for the part, who is a professional actress?*

Well, I'm rather proud of not making mistakes about the people I choose for my films, and – particularly for *The Gospel* – I feel I have always chosen well. The only mistake I've made is this one with Anna Magnani – though the mistake is not really because she is a professional actress. The fact is, if I'd got Anna Magnani to do a *real* petite bourgeoise I would probably have got a good performance out of her; but the trouble is that I didn't get her to do that, I got her to do a woman of the people [*popolana*] with petite bourgeois aspirations, and Anna Magnani just isn't like that. As I choose actors for what they are and not for what they pretend to be, I made a mistake about what the character really was, and although Anna Magnani made a moving effort to do what I asked of her, the character simply did not emerge. I wanted to bring out the ambiguity of subproletarian life with a petit bourgeois superstructure. This didn't come out, because Anna Magnani is a woman who was born and has lived as a petite bourgeoise and then as an actress and so hasn't got those characteristics.

Setting up the con-trick in *Accattone;* and bringing off the con-trick in *Mamma Roma*

How did you find Ettore Garofolo?

That was a bit of luck. I knew his elder brother, who lived in Trastevere. I saw Ettore Garofolo when he was working as a waiter in a restaurant where I went for dinner one evening, Da Meo Patacca, exactly as I showed him in the film, carrying a bowl of fruit just like a figure in a Caravaggio painting. I wrote the script round him, without telling him about it, and then when it was finished I went along there and asked him if he'd like to do it.

Ettore's death is taken from a real event here in Rome, isn't it?

Yes, just about a year before I did the script a young man called Marcello Elisei died just like that.

Did the scene in the film – and the fact that somebody actually died like that in prison – have any effect? Did people react?

Well, it had a bit of effect, but not all that much, because you know things like that happen fairly often in Italy. Just yesterday I saw Parri's denunciation of the police in the papers. These kind of police methods are nothing new. It did have an effect, but in the context of the film as a whole, not as an episode on its own.

The script that you've published in the volume Alì Dagli Occhi Azzurri *is quite different from the script you've used in the film – in fact several of the scripts you've published differ quite a lot from the ones you've used in the films: why is that?*

The script of *Accattone* is almost identical; there's just one episode missing which I had to cut because it was too long. In *Uccellacci e Uccellini*, too, the script is almost the same – there's only one episode missing which I cut because it was too long, but which I shot. So both these are the same, except I cut out a sequence

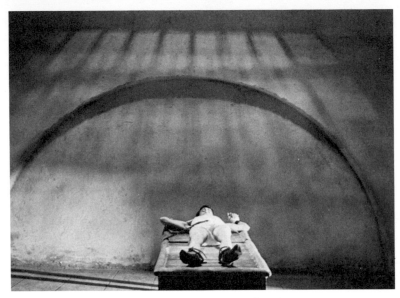

Mamma Roma: Ettore dies on the *letto di contenzione*

because of the length. *Mamma Roma* is different. What happened is that the script was exactly how I shot it, and the changes in the published script I made two or three years after I shot the film, for literary reasons. When I read through the script later I didn't like it – from a literary standpoint – so I changed it.

The critics who complained a lot about the music in Accattone *seem to have digested the music in* Mamma Roma *without much trouble. Do you know why that was?*

I'm not sure. I think what scandalized them in *Accattone* was the mixture of the violent Roman subproletariat with the music of Bach, whereas in *Mamma Roma* there is a different kind of combination which was less shocking – ordinary people who are trying to be petit bourgeois with the music of Vivaldi, which is much

From *Accattone* to *Mamma Roma:* Johann Sebastian Bach and Antonio Vivaldi

more Italian and is based on popular music, so the contamination is much less violent and shocking.

There are two things which weren't quite clear to me. One is when Franco Citti tells Ettore about his mother – this is supposed to demoralize him completely?

Yes, certainly. It gives him an absolute trauma, because he had not lived in a completely subproletarian world. I'll give you an example: in a completely subproletarian world, a world without any bourgeois features, a subproletarian world almost in the sense of a concentration camp, when a boy found out that his mother was a whore he gave her a gold watch so that she would make love with him: perhaps this is a correct reaction in a subproletarian context. Whereas Ettore has been educated by his mother to have

a certain petit bourgeois outlook; he'd been in a college as a child and so finding out his mother was a prostitute gave him a trauma, just like any bourgeois boy finding out something bad about his mother. So he has a collapse, a real crisis, which eventually takes him to his death.

The other thing is that Bruna does not seem quite to belong to the world of the subproletariat like the others.

You could contrast Stella in *Accattone* with Bruna in *Mamma Roma*. Stella is completely immersed in her subproletarian world of poverty, misery and hunger. She lives in a real slum. Whereas if you remember Bruna at a certain moment points out where she lives; when she's going off with Ettore in the middle of the ruins walking down that sort of huge ditch when they're going off to make love she says 'look up there' and points to a large block of flats. Obviously there's TV and the radio and all that in the block of flats. Bruna does belong to the subproletariat inasmuch as there is no real proletariat in Rome to belong to because there is no industry, but it's an upper subproletariat so to speak, a subproletariat at the moment when it is tending to become petit bourgeois and therefore perhaps fascist, conformist, etc., the subproletariat at the moment when it is no longer barricaded inside slums but is exposed to and influenceable by the petit bourgeois and the ruling class through the television, fashion and so on. Bruna is both subproletarian and already corrupted by petit bourgeois influences.

Death is stressed even more in Mamma Roma *than in* Accattone *– and it's a subject you've talked about a good deal in connection with the irrational.*[1]

Death does determine life, I feel that, and I've written it, too, in one of my recent essays, where I compare death to montage. Once life is finished it acquires a sense; up to that point it has not got a sense; its sense is suspended and therefore ambiguous. However,

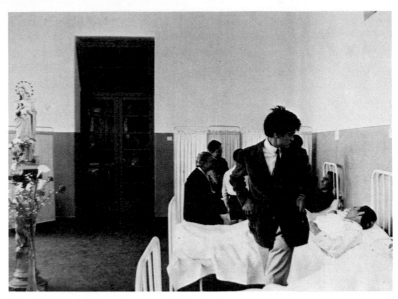

Mamma Roma: Ettore unsuccessfully thieving

to be sincere I must add that for me death is important only if it is not justified and rationalized by reason. For me death is the maximum of epicness and myth. When I'm talking to you about my tendency towards the sacred and the mythic and the epic, I should say that this can only be completely satisfied by the act of death, which seems to me the most mythic and epic aspect there is – all this, however, at a level of pure irrationalism.

In an interview in Image et Son *Barthes says that the cinema should not try to make sense but to suspend sense. Do you agree with that – is it something you've thought much about?*

Yes, that is an old idea of mine, which I've expressed several times ingenuously and crudely when I have said that my films are not supposed to have a finished sense, they always end with a question;

I always intend them to remain suspended. So this thing of Barthes's which I have talked about mostly in connection with Brecht, had already expressed itself, perhaps to some extent unconsciously, in my style and my ideology.

NOTES

1. 'La Paura del Naturalismo', *Nuovi Argomenti* 6 (nuova serie).

La Ricotta: Laura Betti

4: La Ricotta

When you made La Ricotta *were you already thinking of* The Gospel?

Yes; I wrote the script of *La Ricotta* while I was still shooting *Mamma Roma*, but I thought of doing *The Gospel* before I started shooting *La Ricotta* and when I actually shot *La Ricotta* I'd already written the treatment for *The Gospel*, and the initial ideas.

Was Rogopag *conceived as a unit? Was there any relationship between what you did and what Rossellini or Godard did, or did you all just do what you wanted on your own?*

Unfortunately, Bini organized the film his own way. I'd had the idea of doing *La Ricotta* before, with another producer who died. But they had mucked it about because they were afraid; they thought it was too violent. Anyway, I hadn't managed to get the film off the ground and so I found myself with a script ready when Bini asked me if I'd do the film for him. But he'd already decided to make an episode film. So that was that. I didn't have any contact with Rossellini or the others at all, I just knew they were doing episodes as well.

Orson Welles is another professional actor you've used here. How did that go? Who dubbed him, particularly as he had to read one of your poems?

La Ricotta: Stracci on the right →

Well, as I've said, I choose actors for what they really are; I chose Welles for what he is: a director, an intellectual, a man with something of the character which comes out in *La Ricotta*, though, of course, he is a much more complex person than that. It was Giorgio Bassani who did the dubbing.

If you choose actors for what they are, there must be continuity in a character from one film to another – for example, the man who plays the journalist in La Ricotta *is the same person who is conned in* Mamma Roma. *Is that his function – to be conned in* La Ricotta *as well?*

What a person *really* is is something mysterious and profound. The profound, mysterious feature of this man is not that he lets himself be conned, which is typical of a lot of people, particularly ingenuous, kind people; his real profound feature is his vulgarity, which is basically innocent because he doesn't realize what he is. He's just a poor guy, who expresses vulgarity from every pore. I don't think he's either bad or anything else: he's a coward and profoundly vulgar – but innocently so. This is his real quality which I used in both films.

You seem to feel that conformism is an essential feature of the average man – it's one of the words you use in Comizi d'Amore; *when you're talking to the students at Bologna University you try and get them to give a definition of conformism. What do you think it is, and is the essential of the average man not to realize what he is?*

You could say it is the decadence of integration into society. The average man is proud of being what he is and wants everybody else to be the same. He is reductive; he doesn't believe in passion and sincerity, he doesn't believe in people revealing themselves and confessing because the average man is not supposed to do these things. But the other characteristic, equal and opposite, is that this consciousness is not a class consciousness, it's a moralistic, not a political consciousness.

This was the first time you used colour and the pancinor – did you have any trouble?

No, using the zoom is the easiest thing in the world. I just discovered it by chance. I saw you could get certain effects with it, so I used it. Instead of doing a close-up with one kind of lens I did a close-up from a distance with a 250 which gives pictorial effects which I like, which gives a Masaccio-like image. There was no difficulty with the colour because the only difficult thing about colour is selecting out the colours, because there are too many colours in real life. That's why I chose Morocco for *Oedipus*, because there are only a few main colours there – ochre, rose, brown, green, the blue of the sky, only five or six colours for the camera to register. To do a really good colour film you'd need a year or a year and a half to choose the right colours for every image, the ones you really need and not the twenty or thirty colours you always find in the cinema. So *La Ricotta* was easy; I just reproduced exactly the colours used by Pontormo and Rosso Fiorentino.

You had quite a lot of trouble over the film, didn't you? How come you were sentenced to prison?

I was given four months suspended sentence under a fascist law, which is still in force because the magistrates here have never been purged. There are plenty of magistrates who were condemned by anti-fascist courts who are still on the bench. In the fascist code there are a number of crimes of public defamation – including against the nation, the flag and religion. The trial was a kind of farce, and then the sentence was quashed on appeal. I still can't say exactly why they tried me at all, but it was a terrible period for me. I was slandered week after week, and for two or three years I lived under a kind of unimaginable persecution. However, I can't really say why all this happened, unless as an expression of public opinion, which oddly enough, I think is profoundly racist. The Italians are supposed not to be racist, but I think this is a big lie. The Italian bourgeoisie hasn't been racist up to now because it hasn't had the chance. In Libya or Eritrea the ordinary Italian people weren't racist because they were subproletarians from Calabria or Sicily. The petit bourgeoisie didn't have a chance to be racist though they are in fact. I saw this from their attitude to my films. Public opinion rebelled against me because of some indefinable racist hatred, which like all racism was irrational. They couldn't take *Accattone* and all the subproletarian characters. It was racism that provided the basis in public opinion for the trial to be possible.

Was La Ricotta *banned for good in Italy?*

It was banned for a while after the trial and the film was confiscated, then I was able to bring it out with a few small cuts like somebody shouting 'away with the crosses' (when the director in the film wanted to shoot another scene): this was considered anti-Catholic. But it wasn't a success because, as you know, if a film doesn't come out at the right time it has had it.

5: Comizi d'Amore and La Rabbia

I've just seen Comizi d'Amore: *why did you decide to make this kind of film? How did it do in Italy? And why did it never go abroad?*

It had absolutely no success at all in Italy. It only came out in a few 'art' cinemas and I don't think it ever went abroad because it did so badly in Italy. Anyway, there would have been a big translation problem: you'd lose the accents and the dialects, and the jokes: it would be impossible to dub it and sub-titles would make it too cold. Someone who didn't know Italian properly could not take the film in; he could only see it as a purely sociological event, not as something cinematographic, he would only be able to get the *sense* of the answers, not their feeling. At least it would need a highly specialized public, which is what it got in Italy in any case, it was only cinephiles and sociologists who went to see it.

Do you know why that was? Was it for the reasons which Moravia and Musatti talk about in the film[1] – fear and so on?

I don't think so; I think the basic reason is much more banal than that. It's simply that the public saw themselves reflected too faith-fully. The ideological and social world that Italians live in only becomes meaningful to someone who is outside it; all people living in it saw was their own everyday life reproduced.

65

Cesare Musatti: he subsequently denounced the methods and the results of *Comizi d'Amore* as reactionary

But the soldier who says 'It's the society that forces us to be Don Juans' demonstrates an awareness of social pressures – surely he is similarly representative of the public?

When the soldier says 'society' he means his family circle and his immediate milieu. He's using the word 'society' in a very special way. When you say the film reflects Italian society you're seeing it from the outside, as I do now because I've succeeded in detaching myself; but the average Italian, who has no deep awareness of the world, no real social consciousness, does not realize what's going on. He feels immersed in the film like in everyday life.

The strongest impression I got from watching the film was a powerful drive among the people you talked with towards straightforward repression of anything they didn't understand – particularly homo-

sexuality. Did you follow this up at all? Was there any more material on this which you didn't use?

There was a bit more, but very much the same. One or two people in Sicily spoke with more sincerity and violence, but the material in the film is quite representative. Ordinary Italian people are not very repressed, from a sexual point of view; in fact they are very free. If you want to talk to the ordinary people about sex you can do so extremely freely. The petit bourgeoisie, on the other hand, is naturally repressed, like everywhere, but it is basically not a very sincere repression, it isn't very much felt; it's rather superficial. Repression is not so pathological as it is in other bourgeois societies which don't have Catholicism, which is basically not a rigid religion. There hasn't been a Protestant revolution in Italy, in fact in a sense there hasn't been a religious revolution at all: Catholicism has superimposed itself on paganism, particularly among the ordinary people, without changing them in the slightest.

But in England, which has had a Protestant revolution, most physical violence is located inside the family – and you've certainly got the family in Italy. What about violence there?

Yes, the family is the nest of convention, certainly. I'm a bit surprised that it still is in England because basically the family is a pre-industrial institution. The industrially advanced societies are beginning not to need the family any more. The family was a nucleus of conservation in agrarian society, but now I think that in America, for example, it is beginning to have much less importance.

Recently Maurizio Ponzi made a 'crito-film'[2] on your style, and he chose the end of Comizi d'Amore *to exemplify his theses, the bit about the wedding where you read one of your poems. I gather he chose this piece to demonstrate that the crucial factor in your films is montage. Do you agree with this?*

It is an atrocious dilemma. For a long time I thought the crucial factor was what the French call *l'action profilmique* i.e. everything

Comizi d'Amore: children in the Palermo slums, and Neapolitan women

Comizi d'Amore: the Bologna football team, and Antonella Lualdi

that happens in front of the camera and which I represent. At other times I have been led to think that the crucial thing is the montage, because the duration of an image is of fundamental importance – if I see something for half a minute it has one value, if I see it for three minutes it has another. So I am very uncertain.

I think Ponzi has made a fine film: it is a remarkable attempt at cinema criticism. I think the reason he chose that piece from *Comizi d'Amore* was because it was an average, representative example of my style which was fairly successful, in which the montage is certainly important, but not excessively so.

What do you feel about La Rabbia?

La Rabbia is a strange film because it is entirely made up of documentary material, I didn't shoot a single frame. Mainly it's pieces from newsreels, so the material is extremely banal and down-right reactionary. I chose some sequences from newsreels of the late fifties and put them together my own way – they're mostly about the Algerian War, the reign of Pope John, and there are a few minor episodes like the return of the Italian prisoners of war from Russia. My criterion was, let's say, that of a marxist denunciation of the society of the time, and what was happening in it. One odd thing about the film is that the commentary is in verse: I wrote some poetry specially for it, and it is read by Giorgio Bassani, who dubbed Orson Welles in *La Ricotta*, and by the painter Renato Guttuso. The best thing in my half of the film, and the only bit that is worth keeping, is the sequence devoted to the death of Marilyn Monroe.

The film came to a bad end, didn't it, because of Guareschi's part?[3]

It's not a very interesting story. I did my episode, thinking that was all there was to it, but when I'd finished the producer decided he wanted to have a commercial hit and so he had the brilliant idea of getting another episode with a commentary from the other side of the political spectrum. However, the person he chose,

Comizi d'Amore: the bridegroom and his mother; Giovanni Guareschi

Guareschi, was unacceptable. So there was some trouble with the producer, and anyway the film was a flop because people weren't interested in such highly political material.

NOTES

1. In the film, Pasolini discusses his project with Moravia and Musatti before starting and then again half-way through when they have had a chance to examine some of his material.
2. *Il cinema di Pasolini* (13 mins). For a discussion of this film, see Luigi Faccini, 'Una ipotesi cinematografico di linguaggio critico', *Cinema e Film* 1.
3. The film was blocked after popular outcry against what seemed like racism in Giovanni Guareschi's portion. Unfortunately, the distributors (Warners) exploited the occasion to bury the entire film for good. Giovanni Guareschi is, sadly, famous abroad for his wretched Don Camillo books.

6: Sopraluoghi in Palestina and The Gospel According to St Matthew

When you made Sopraluoghi in Palestina *did you envisage showing it in public, or was it initially conceived as a private research film?*

It came about very casually, and in fact I never took any part in the camera set-ups or the shooting or anything else. When we went to the Middle East there was a cameraman with us who was sent along by the production company. I never suggested a thing to him, because I wasn't thinking of using the material to make a film, I just wanted some documentation which would help me set *The Gospel*. When I got back to Rome the producer asked me to put together some of the footage and put a commentary on it so it could be shown to a few distributors and Christian Democrat bosses to help the producers. I didn't even control the montage. I had it put together by someone and then just looked over it, but I left everything, including some very ugly cuts which this person had made – who anyway wasn't even a qualified editor. I had it put on in a dubbing-room and improvised a commentary, so altogether the whole film is rather improvised.

The conversations between you and Don Andrea must have been done at the time.

Yes, those are real, but it was the cameraman who decided whether or not to record them.

Sopraluoghi in Palestina: 'These won't do for the film'; 'I realized it was all no use'

74

After the business with La Ricotta *you must have had some trouble re-establishing good relations with representatives of the Church?*

I had good relations with Don Giovanni Rossi and the others from the Pro Civitate Christiana organization and with some other people from the Catholic left, let's say, before the *La Ricotta* affair. But everything was made easier by the advent of Pope John XXIII who objectively revolutionized the situation. If Pius XII had lived another three or four years I'd never have been able to make *The Gospel*.

One thing that seemed a bit odd to me in Sopraluoghi *is where you meet some Arab children and you say something like 'These won't do for the film because you can see that Christ's preaching has not passed across their faces'; I didn't quite get this.*

That's a bit difficult to explain because it is one of those things which come from the heart. But historically it is true – you can't say it isn't. It's something I said from inspiration, yet at the same time it is something banal; it is true in the most practical and brutal sense of the word, just as it is true of the Italians in Southern Italy – you can see that Christ's preaching hasn't passed by there either because their morality is not evangelical, it isn't founded on love but on honour; there's no pietism; there isn't even piety at bottom, in the Christian sense of the word – i.e. in the slightly blackmailing sense. If there is piety it's because it's there, not because it is supposed to be there. You can see this better in the Arabs than in Southern Italians.

How long did it take you to realize there was nothing you could use? In the film I think it's Don Andrea Carraro who says it first, but one gets the distinct impression that you'd been feeling it before that.

When I landed at Tel Aviv, naturally, I couldn't make out anything. It was night-time. All I could see was an airport and a city. I got a car and went in towards the interior. Right at the beginning I got a few images of an ancient world, which was mainly Arab. I thought at first I might be able to use them, but then immediately afterwards the kibbutzim began to appear, and reafforestation works, modern agriculture, light industry, etc. and I realized it was all no use – that was after a few hours driving.

Recently, after the June War you published[1] some poems which you wrote while you were in Palestine but didn't publish at the time, along with a text about Israel which was more or less an attack on L'Unità. It's a bit difficult to see from these what you thought of Israel as a society: what did you think of it?

The poems in *Nuovi Argomenti* are poems I didn't include in *Poesia in Forma di Rosa*, where there's a section called 'Israel' which gives an idea of the impression the society gave me: it's a contradictory one, in the sense that I disapprove of it fundamentally because it's founded on a basically racist, messianic and religious idea – the idea of a promised land based on religious reasons which go back three thousand years, which is all completely mad. I don't accept the premise, which is a nationalistic-religious one – it's horrible, although it's basically the same principle on which all states are based. But on this premise has been built a nation which inspires great sympathy – for example, the kibbutzim although they are profoundly sad and recall the concentration camps and the Jews' tendency towards masochism and self-exclusion are at the same time something extremely noble, one of the most democratic and socially advanced experiments I've ever seen. Moreover, I have always loved the Jews because they have been excluded, because they are objects of racial hatred, because they have been forced to be separate from society. But once they've founded their own state they are not different, they're not a minority, they're not excluded: they are the majority, they are the norm. And that was a bit of a disappointment, I don't quite know how to put it. They, who had always been the champions of difference, of martyrdom, of the fight of the other against the normal had now become the majority and the normal and that was something I found it a bit hard to swallow.

Who controls things like changing the title of a film – because you presumably know Il Vangelo Secondo Matteo *was changed in England, as was the dedication to John XXIII?*[2]

That's something I wonder about myself, with considerable anguish I must say. I don't know what to do about this kind of thing. I'd like to know how you do find out, because I feel completely helpless.

From what you've said about your upbringing Catholicism is not something inside you, it's something with which you have chosen to have a relationship, which is mainly an external relationship: it's a factor in Italian society rather than a factor in you – is that a fair way of looking at why you chose this text for a film?

Well, if you saw *The Gospel* as a work of a practising Catholic then you're right to put me the question. But I don't think that is right. Maybe I didn't realize this even myself until a month ago when I saw it again after a gap of two or three years. It's not a practising Catholic work, it seems to me an unpleasant and terrible work, at certain points outright ambiguous and disconcerting, particularly the figure of Christ. It's only externally that the film has the characteristic features of a Catholic work. But internally nothing I've ever done has been more fitted to me myself than *The Gospel* for the reasons I talked about before – my tendency always to see something sacred and mythic and epic in everything, even the most humdrum, simple and banal objects and events. So in this sense *The Gospel* was just right for me, even though I don't believe in the divinity of Christ, because my vision of the world is religious – it's a mutilated religion because it hasn't got any of the external characteristics of religion, but it is a religious vision of the world, so making *The Gospel* was to reach the maximum of the mythic and the epic. Besides, the whole film is full of my own personal motifs – e.g. all the minor characters from the agricultural and pastoral proletariat of Southern Italy are mine completely,[3] and I only realized this when I saw it again now; and I also realized that the Christ figure is all mine, because of the terrible ambiguity there is in him.

How in fact did you choose the figure for Christ?

That was a sudden inspiration involving psychological factors in me, my way of seeing people. I spent more than a year looking everywhere for someone to do Christ, and I'd almost decided to use a German actor. And then one day I came back to the house and found this young Spaniard, Enrique Irazoqui, sitting here waiting to see me and as soon as I saw him, even before he had a chance to start talking, I said: 'Excuse me, but would you act in one of my films?' – even before I knew who he was or anything. He was a serious person, and so he said 'no'. But then I gradually won him round.

I've seen somewhere that you were thinking of using a poet for Christ – the two names mentioned were Kerouac and Yevtushenko: that seems a bit odd?

These were just possibilities. As I thought of representing Christ as an intellectual in a world of the poor available for revolution and as I was looking for an analogy between what Christ really was and the person who might interpret him, I felt the only real possibility would be to use a poet; so I went through all the poets and two who held my attention for a moment were Yevtushenko and Kerouac, but then I discovered that the photograph of Kerouac was ten or fifteen years out of date – but these were only two of many I considered for a moment.

What about the apostles: in an interview you once said you chose intellectuals because that was the only analogy you could find?

No, I chose the apostles according to whatever information we had about them. Some of them were from the people, like Peter who was a fisherman, so he was done by a young Jewish subproletarian from Rome – about half of them were from humble origins; others, like Matthew, did have a more intellectual background, so I chose an intellectual for him.

The trouble about making a film of the Gospel is that it isn't just any old story, it's a story that in a society like Italy has been captured by an institution, the Catholic Church. It is difficult to read the Gospel, in an Althusserian sense; and a film on the subject surely runs the risk of becoming, likewise, the property of the Church as an institution, in this particular cultural situation.

Yes, I agree, this was a real danger, but you must also bear in mind that nobody in Italy reads the Gospel, really nobody. I asked every single person I knew and only three or four at the most had read the Gospel, so that this was much less of a danger in Italy than elsewhere – in fact making a film about the Gospel meant suggesting to the Italians that they read the Gospel for the first time. Otherwise this would have been a greater danger in a country like England where the Gospel is widely read. In fact the film had a different reception in Italy from what it got in England and America: in Italy it was a disconcerting and scandalous novelty, because no one expected a Christ like that, because no one had read Matthew's Gospel; whereas in England and America it confirmed people's viewpoint, by and large; it certainly wasn't considered scandalous.

What did you mean when you said that the text was the only one you'd come across which had a 'moral beauty'?[4]

That's another of my inspirational remarks which are difficult to explain, partly because they are a bit rhetorical. That was a moment of literary crisis: many people up to that time had had a certain code of aesthetic criteria which they then lost because Italian culture was in a state of crisis. I think what I meant was

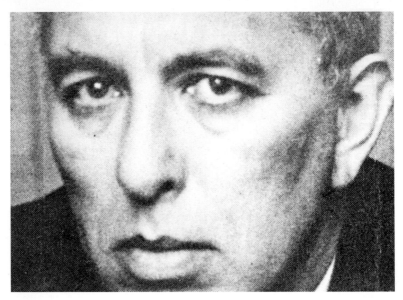

Franco Fortini: contributor to Italian rationalism

that beauty was no longer recognizable as an aesthetic fact, but as a moral one.

You also said that the film was partly the product of a reflux of irrationalism in yourself – but this is a phenomenon which it is extremely difficult to accommodate within the tradition of Italian culture, which has distinguished itself by its rejection of both irrationalism and rationalism, so for cultural reasons as well as just immediately religious ones you had a major problem of expression.

Well, yes, you're right about Italian culture. All the same, in the last few years there has been a certain dialectic between rationalism and irrationalism. All the pre-war culture, hermeticism and so on, was completely irrationalistic: it substituted ratiocination for reason, but it was still irrational.

The post-war period produced a flood of sentimentalism, with

Matera: the *Sassi*

the discovery of everyday humdrum life and all that. Yet along
with this there was also the first serious rethinking of a rationalist-
ideological kind, and I think I can fairly say that this coincided
with the review *Officina*, which was founded by me and several
friends of mine, Leonetti, Roversi, Fortini and others in the mid
fifties. *Officina* provided the first critical revision of a rationalist
kind of neo-realism and of the whole of Italian literature, naturally
in a fairly sporadic and fragmentary way. This rationalism had
marxist origins, but with heterodox tendencies, and although it
had marxist origins it was very much in polemic with the Communist Party, which tended to give in too much to a certain kind
of sentimentalism; it was too soft on the Vatican (like agreeing to
keep the Concordat), at a time when the Vatican was terrifically
reactionary, and the whole place was crawling with fascists.

You found some good locations – where were they?

The whole film was shot in Southern Italy. I had decided to do this even before I went to Palestine, which I only did to set my conscience at ease. I knew I would remake the Gospel by analogy. Southern Italy enabled me to make the transposition from the ancient to the modern world without having to reconstruct it either archaeologically or philologically. I did a long tour of the South alone by car and chose all the locations and then went back with my assistants and did the planning.

Where was Jerusalem, for example?

That was the old part of Matera, which now, alas, is falling into ruin, the part known as the *Sassi*. Bethlehem was a village in Apulia called Barile, where people were really living in caves, like in the film, only a few years ago. The castles were Norman castles dotted round Apulia and Lucania. The desert part where Christ is walking along with the apostles I shot in Calabria. And Capernaum is made up of two towns: the part down by the sea is a village near Crotone, and the part looking away from the sea is Massafra.

On the whole the critics reckoned you were successful with this attempt to film the Gospel by analogy rather than reconstruction, but one of the elements that is omitted is any reference to the political context. From what you've said about your St Paul project it sounds as though you will handle it slightly differently. Do you accept any of the criticism along this line?

The fact that I made the film by analogy means that I was not interested in exactitude. I was interested in everything but that. Obviously, I have left out objectively important political and social factors. By nature I adopted a definite position in my reconstruction: in a choice between an exact reproduction of Palestine two thousand years ago and getting close to present-day reality, I would choose the latter. Besides, along with this method of reconstruction by analogy, there is the idea of the myth and of epicness which I have talked about so much: so when I told the story of Christ I didn't reconstruct Christ as he really was. If I had reconstructed the history of Christ as he really was I would not have produced a religious film because I am not a believer. I don't believe Christ is the son of God. I would have produced a positivist or marxist reconstruction at the most, and thus at best a life which could have been the life of any one of the five or six thousand saints there were preaching at that time in Palestine. But I did not want to do this, because I am not interested in de-consecrating: this is a fashion I hate, it is petit bourgeois. I want to re-consecrate things as much as possible, I want to re-mythicize them. I did not want to reconstruct the life of Christ as it really was, I wanted to do the story of Christ plus two thousand years of Christian translation, because it is the two thousand years of Christian history which have mythicized this biography, which would otherwise be an almost insignificant biography as such. My film is the life of Christ plus two thousand years of story-telling about the life of Christ. That was my intention.

It was precisely this problem of making a film of a text by a believer when you yourself are not a believer which created considerable practical and theoretical trouble for you – and helped stimulate some of your theories about the cinema, I think.

Very briefly, this is what happened. Already in *Accattone* my style was religious – I thought it was (although I prefer the word 'reverential' [*sacrale*]), and all the critics thought it was, though they called it 'Catholic' rather than 'religious', which was wrong. But it was religious in the style rather than the content: it is possible to cheat in the content, but you can't cheat in the style. When I started *The Gospel* I thought I had the right formula all ready, and I started out shooting it with the same techniques and style as I used for *Accattone*. But after two days I was in a complete crisis and I even contemplated giving the whole thing up, which had never happened to me in my whole life, except for this time. Using a reverential style for *The Gospel* was gilding the lily: it came out rhetoric. Reverential technique and style in *Accattone* went fine,

The Gospel: Piero della Francesca Pharisees; (opposite) taking a break

but applied to a sacred text they were ridiculous; so I got dis-
couraged and was just about to give the whole thing up, and then
when I was shooting the baptism scene near Viterbo I threw over
all my technical preconceptions. I started using the zoom, I used
new camera movements, new frames which were not reverential,
but almost documentary. A completely new style emerged. In
Accattone the style is consistent and extremely simple, like in
Masaccio or in Romanesque sculpture. Whereas the style in *The
Gospel* is very varied: it combines the reverential with almost
documentary moments, an almost classic severity with moments
that are almost Godardian – e.g., the two trials of Christ shot like
cinéma vérité. The same contrast between the styles of *Accattone*
and *The Gospel* comes out in the references to painting: in *Accattone* there is only one figurative element – Masaccio, perhaps deep
down Giotto and Romanesque sculpture as well, but anyway only
one *type* of reference; whereas in *The Gospel* there are numerous

different sources – Piero della Francesca (in the Pharisees' clothes), Byzantine painting (Christ's face like a Rouault), etc. Recently I saw an exhibition of Rouault's work with some paintings of Christ where he had exactly the same face as my Christ. Anyway, there are numerous references. And that goes for the music as well: the music in *The Gospel* is a mixture of different styles and techniques.

The point is that in *Accattone* I was telling the story in the first person, in *The Gospel* I was not telling the story in the same way: I, a non-believer, was telling the story through the eyes of a believer. This mixture at the narrative level produced the mixture stylistically.

Was the change of technique during the shooting of the baptism partly due to technical difficulties, like the terrain?

No, it was voluntary. I spent one completely sleepless night and then decided to give it up, but then when I went out in the morning I just decided to revolutionize everything: this was a big decision for me, because I was not a professional, in fact I knew nothing at all about cinema techniques when I started *Accattone*, not even what the different lenses were and things like that.

Is there anything left of the footage you shot before the change?

Yes, there's Gethsemane and the sermon on the mount. I tried to salvage both these during the montage, but they are not right and I don't like them.

It is curious that though there are a lot of references to painting and cinema in the film, the end result is surprisingly consistent. You used to say you could not explain this – can you explain it now?

No, I'm still surprised; obviously I fooled myself. But anyway by mixture of styles I don't mean a random mixture, I mean an amalgam. Clearly the film has a stylistic unity, but it is not to be found in any one single formula, it is a mixture of various formulae. I have never said there is no stylistic unity: the unity comes from a mixture of styles.

The first time I saw the film just after I'd finished it, I thought it did have stylistic unity, and this surprised me; and then I realized this was because I had told the story myself, and therefore I probably do believe after all. The stylistic unity is only my own unconscious religiousness, which came out and gave the film its unity. Then I saw the film again just a month or two ago and I changed my mind about it again: it is not true that it has stylistic unity. What happened was that when I was shooting the film I was changing ideas the whole time and trying out new things like hand-held camera, *cinéma vérité* and so on, and so I expected it to look very varied; then when I saw it just after I'd finished it it was much less of a hotch-potch than I expected. But when I saw it again just now the internal dramatic nature came out which I'd missed the first time. It is a violently contradictory film, profoundly ambiguous and disconcerting, particularly the figure of Christ – at times he is almost embarrassing, as well as being enigmatic. There are some horrible moments I am ashamed of, which are almost Counter-Reformation Baroque, repellent – the miracles. The miracles of the loaves and the fishes and Christ walking on the water are disgusting pietism. The jump from these kind of holy picture scenes to the passionate violence of his politics and his preaching is so great that the Christ figure in the film is bound to produce a strong sense of unease in an audience. Catholics come out of the film a bit shaken up feeling that I have made Christ bad. He is not bad in fact, he is just full of contradictions.

He is full of contradictions in the text, too.

In this case I have done a kind of analogy involuntarily. I have reconstructed, by analogy, in a modern figure the teleological contradictions there are in the Gospel. The Gospel is full of contradictions. They are essential; they are what make it great and

The Gospel: Salome's dance

The Gospel: Christ is crowned with thorns

rich. But while the contradictions in the text are contradictions of content, of meaning, passion, faith, religion, the contradictions in my film are more existential and therefore more disquieting.

To go back to the miracles. Some of these read quite nicely in the text, but they jar in the film. It is noticeable, though, that the miracle in La Terra vista dalla Luna *comes off much better. Why do you think that is?*

It is very simple. In my case, everything has to be real, even if only by analogy. I did the miracles with artificial aids, and you can see them. If I could have got Enrique Irazoqui really to walk on the water, even hypnotized, it would have been stupendous. The other point is that we live in a culture which does not believe in miracles, and so they have an unpleasant effect on us but this is not true for a Southern Italian peasant who is still living in a magical culture where miracles are real like the culture in which Matthew wrote, and so perhaps he wouldn't notice the device.

This is one point where there is an insoluble contradiction between what you are doing and what Matthew was doing. The combination breaks down on the miracles.

Because for everything else I was able to find an analogy. Perhaps I should have tried to invent completely new miracles, miracles which are not miracles, like healing or walking on the water; perhaps I should have tried to convey the sense of miraculousness each of us can experience watching the dawn, for example: nothing happens, the sun rises, trees are lit up by the sun. Perhaps for us this is what a miracle is. But I didn't think about it at the time, and now I'm only groping around. In *La Terra vista dalla Luna* the key was surrealism, which makes the whole thing a miracle.

What will you do in St Paul?

There won't be any. All there will be will be some con men pretending to perform miracles, who are then severely punished by St Paul. This will be set in Southern Italy somewhere between Naples and Rome.

You don't feel you ever loaded too much on to Matthew's text – for example the references to painting?

No, I think they came out all right, as the final unity shows. You do notice them, but I don't find them irritating. Besides, as I have said, I wanted to do the story of Christ plus two thousand years of Christianity. At least for an Italian like me painting has had an enormous importance in these two thousand years, indeed it is the major element in the Christological tradition.

When I first saw the film I thought you were making a very strong critique from within: the opening sequences seem to be of two people

The Gospel: crowds listening to Christ; *Oedipus Rex:* crowds following Franco Citti

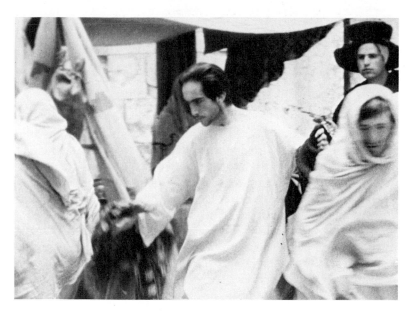

The Gospel: Christ in the temple

who just don't know what's happening to them; likewise when Christ comes down from the mountain and passes the group of peasants, he just shouts at them so they don't have a chance to understand what he's saying. Then gradually, it seemed to me, as the film advances, you drop this approach.

This was deliberate. But the first images of Mary and Joseph are different: these are two earthly creatures to whom something monstrously divine is happening, which they are not equal to. There is an obvious disproportion between them and the celestial powers which are descending to them. But basically this is only an intensification of the spiritual element there is in all innocence: any innocent young girl is full of mystery, all I tried to do was to multiply a thousandfold the mystery in this young girl. The use of disproportion, people being unprepared for the confrontation with divine events, is deliberate. I shot Christ's first phrase to the peasants like that because I wanted to give a crescendo to his preaching. As you remember, he starts out walking almost alone. Roberto Longhi said something very beautiful about this scene; he said he liked it because Christ was going out into the country with the impetus and the sense of a future full of things to do just like a nineteenth-century impressionist would have gone out to paint in the open air.

You continued this stylistic approach, because in many of his harshest speeches against the Pharisees there are huge crowds, and then for some of the sermons Catholics find most important he is talking to almost nobody.

Yes, all that is because I thought the people round him, like Matthew himself, considered these earthly speeches about the problem of the Jewish people and so on more important than the purely theological and metaphysical sermons. Basically, Matthew is the most earthly of all the evangelists.

Is that why you chose him?

Yes, and because he is the most revolutionary; he is the nearest to the real problems of an historical epoch. Personally, I like John's Gospel even more, but I thought Matthew's was the best for making a film.

When you say Matthew is the most revolutionary, you surely know that many people consider him the most counter-*revolutionary of the evangelists: that his main point was to convince the Jews to back Christ, who was a moderate, against the Pharisees who were the religious leaders of the national liberation struggle.*[5]

I was not interested in reconstructing the whole situation exactly. It is the feeling of the Gospel as a whole when you first read it that is revolutionary. Christ going round Palestine is really a revolutionary whirlwind: someone who walks up to a couple of people and says 'drop your nets and follow me' is a total revolutionary. Subsequently, of course, you may go into it more thoroughly, historically and textually, but the first reading is profoundly revolutionary.

What about the text – for example, the Our Father is the truncated Catholic version, isn't it?

I deliberately followed a standard Catholic translation to avoid useless polemics.

Is the language accessible to an average Italian?

It is slightly antiquated, but it would not seem strange to an average Italian because they are used to religion being in that kind of language: it is normal, like the language on the television.

You have put in one or two bits that aren't in Matthew like the text when Christ dies.

Yes, that is from Isaiah. That is one of the few liberties I allowed myself. There is another bit from Isaiah where he is walking along

The Gospel: on the way to Gethsemane

with the apostles in Calabria just before the investiture of Peter.
But the whole of Matthew is full of quotes from Isaiah, so I felt
that was fair enough.

*Am I right in thinking the investiture of Peter wasn't in the original
version?*

I shot it with the rest of the film, but then removed it after the first
editing. But this caused such grief to my friends in the Pro Civitate
Christiana that I put it back again. It was an act of kindness
towards my Catholic friends.

Did you shoot much more that you didn't use?

I shot enough to make a film of about $2\frac{1}{2}$ to $2\frac{3}{4}$ hours – all Christ's
eschatological sermons, and some other bits like the Gadarene

swine, for example, which I removed because it was really horrible. In Italy you have to put at least two students from the Centro Sperimentale [Film School] into every film, so I got them to do the people possessed by devils, but you could see they were students from the film school, the reality came out, it was awful, so I got rid of it.

You know that a lot of left-wing intellectuals did not like the film. Sciascia[6] described you as the seismograph of the dialogue. Fortini said the film was an instrument of the dialogue. Do you mind?

The point is that I have contributed to the dialogue. I am not the seismograph of it, I haven't just registered it, I have helped to produce it, and I think I was right to do so. When I first started to do so no one was thinking about it, you must understand that. It was not a fashionable occupation, I was not exploiting a fashion, though I knew this might become a danger, and indeed after a while I stopped talking about it. I said my bit and then shut up. I did not join the chorus of those exploiting the dialogue. However, I still think I was right. Groups of Catholics have now emerged on the left of the PCI – the phenomenon of Don Milani, the Catholic left: these are very important phenomena for Italy. These have already transcended the exploitation of the dialogue, which if anything is now taking place between Paul VI and the communists (in a highly contradictory way, of course), but I'm not interested in that. What I am interested in is the emergence of advanced Catholics like Don Milani, so I cannot feel that my efforts towards the dialogue were fruitless.

NOTES

1. In *Nuovi Argomenti* 6 (nuova serie). *L'Unità* is the PCI daily.
2. The English distributors introduced 'St' into the title, against Pasolini's express intentions. Likewise the word 'joyful' (*lieta*) was cut from the dedication to John XXIII.
3. Some of Pasolini's friends figure in the film: the poet Alfonso Gatto as Andrew; the critic Enzo Siciliano as Simon of Canaan; Natalia Ginzburg, the novelist, as Mary of Bethany; Elsa Morante's brother Marcello as Joseph.

4. *Film Comment,* Fall 1965.
5. On this, see the excellent article by José L. Serrano, 'Contra "El Evangelio según San Mateo" ', *Temas de Cine* 37; cf. Felix Martialay, 'El falso prestigio de Pier Paolo Pasolini, un director "bruciato" ', *Film Ideal* 17 May 1965; and M. Casolaro, S. J., 'Spirito e lettera nel film di Pier Paolo Pasolini', *Cineforum* 40, for an intelligent orthodox Catholic view.
6. Leonardo Sciascia is a Sicilian novelist, author of several fine works set in Sicily: among them *Il Giorno della Civetta, Il Consiglio d'Egitto,* and *Gli Zii di Sicilia.*

7: Uccellacci e Uccellini

You changed style with Uccellacci e Uccellini, *too: initially, it was supposed to be what you called an 'ideo-comic' film, but it didn't exactly come out like that.*

Well, I don't know, perhaps it came out too much like that: too 'ideo' and not 'comic' enough (anyway that was a formula I just invented for fun, it's not a serious category). As for the change of style, I think I have a basic style which I will always have: there is a basic continuity from *Accattone* onwards through *The Gospel*, which is obviously part of my psychology and my pathology, which as you know is unchangeable (even *Theorem*, which I was going to shoot in a completely different way, has come out with analogous features to the others). In *Uccellacci e Uccellini* I think the new element was that I tried to make it more cinema – there are almost no references to the figurative arts, and many more explicit references to other films. *Uccellacci e Uccellini* is the product of a cinematographic rather than a figurative culture, unlike *Accattone*. It is about the end of neo-realism as a kind of limbo, and it evokes the ghost of neo-realism, particularly the beginning about two characters living out their life without thinking about it – i.e. two typical heroes of neo-realism, humble, humdrum and unaware. All the first part is an evocation of neo-realism, though naturally an idealized neo-realism. There are other bits like the clowns episode which are deliberately intended to evoke

Uccellacci e Uccellini: Totò and Ninetto Davoli, and the crow

Fellini and Rossellini.[1] Some critics accused me of being Fellinian in that episode, but they did not understand that it was a quotation from Fellini; in fact immediately afterwards the crow talks to the two of them and says 'The age of Brecht and Rossellini is finished.' The whole episode was a long quotation.

You don't think the critics got confused between what you were saying and what the crow was saying?

I don't think so, because the crow is extremely autobiographical: there is almost total identity between me and the crow.

How did you fix the crow?

That crow was a really wild mad beast and it nearly drove all the rest of us mad as well. In fact, one of the comic sketches I thought of doing was one where Totò and Ninetto would be the owners of a crow like this, because it was an enormous struggle, the toughest fight of my life. Generally a director's main worry in Italy is the sun, because the weather in Rome is very unreliable. But after the weather my biggest worry was this crow. The bits there are with it in the film I managed to get together only by shooting again and again and then organizing the montage very carefully, but it was a terrible ordeal. Then the crow died, which upset Ninetto a great deal, so when he went to India and saw all the crows there he felt he was among friends again because a kind of *omertà* had been established between him and the crows.

How about Totò? You took a chance using him, because he was already a famous comic actor in Italy, but very much a typed actor. Do you think he was too much associated with a certain character in the Italian mind – though to an outsider he was fine?

I chose Totò for what he was – an actor, a recognizable type whom the public already knew. I didn't want him to be anything but what he was. Poor Totò, he used to ask me very gently, almost like a child, if he could make a more serious film, and I used to have to say 'No, no, I just want you to be yourself.' The real Totò was in fact manipulated, he wasn't a straightforward ingenuous character like Franco Citti in *Accattone*. Totò was an actor who had been manipulated by himself and by other people into a type, but I used him precisely as that, as someone who was a type. He was a strange mixture of credulousness and popular Neapolitan authenticity on the one hand and of a clown on the other – i.e. recognizable and neo-realist and also slightly absurd and surreal. That is why I chose him, and that is what he was, even in the worst films he ever made.

How did you find Ninetto Davoli?

I met him by chance when I was making *La Ricotta* – he was there with a whole lot of other boys watching us making the film and I

Uccellacci e Uccellini: 'Totò and Ninetto Davoli are a very normal father and son'; 'they clash with new historical situations'

noticed him at once because of his curly hair and his character which later came out in my film. When I thought of doing *Uccellacci e Uccellini* I thought of him and Totò at once without the slightest hesitation. I gave him a tiny part as a shepherd boy in *The Gospel*, as a kind of screen-test.

I thought it was strange that you chose a father-son relationship, which is not simply one of generations but also one of family linearity, to illustrate a major ideological shift.

But Totò and Ninetto are a very normal father and son, there is no great clash between them, they are perfectly in agreement with each other, they embody a type which perpetuates itself: Ninetto is like Totò, there is this combination of total humdrumness and something magical in both of them. There is no conflict of generations between them. The son is getting ready to be an ordinary man just like his father was, with some differences like wearing different clothes. He will probably go and work at Fiat's, but whatever the different characteristics are they will not become consciousness, they will not become a cause of disagreement or rivalry with his father.

I don't quite follow that – is that the thesis of the film or the thesis you are criticizing?

Totò and Ninetto are mankind, and as such both old and new. What they clash with are new historical situations, but as mankind they are not in contradiction with each other.

But take Togliatti's death, for example, which plays a big part in the film:[2] this did not mark a great change in Italian life, as far as I can see.

No, in itself it did not, but it symbolized a change. A historical epoch, the epoch of the Resistance, of great hopes for communism, of the class struggle, has finished. What we have now is the

economic boom, the welfare state, and industrialization which is using the South as a reserve of cheap manpower and even beginning to industrialize it as well. There has been a real change which coincided more or less with Togliatti's death. It was a pure coincidence chronologically, but it worked symbolically.

But in that context the generation break is surely what is most important, because the communism of the Resistance and anti-fascism in particular is something which has been kept alive artificially by the older generation in the Party: anti-fascism is something they should have transcended.

I agree: the feeling of the Resistance and the class struggle have outlived themselves rather, but this is something which involves the Central Committee and the leadership of the Communist Party, i.e. a particular group, whereas Totò and Ninetto represent the mass of Italians who are outside all that – the innocent Italians who are around us, who are not involved in history, who are just acquiring the very first iota of consciousness; that is when they encounter marxism, in the shape of the crow.

But straight after Togliatti's funeral they meet the girl by the road-side – i.e. once communism is finished (or this epoch is over) they immediately go off with a woman.

Well, no. The woman represents vitality. Things die and we feel grief, but then vitality comes back again – that's what the woman represents. In fact, the story of Togliatti does not end there, because after they have been off with the woman there is the crow again. They perform an act of cannibalism, what Catholics call communion: they swallow the body of Togliatti (or of the marxists) and assimilate it; after they have assimilated it they carry on along the road, so that even though you don't know where the road is going, it is obvious that they have assimilated marxism.

There is a certain ambiguity about it: it is both destruction and consumption.

← *Uccellacci e Uccellini:* Totò and Femi Benussi: 'the woman represents vitality'

Yes, that's what it's meant to be. Just before the crow is eaten he says 'Teachers are made to be eaten in *salsa piccante.*' They must be eaten and transcended, but if their teaching is of any value it remains inside us.

What about the first sequence, which you first tried to cut down, and then finally removed altogether?[3]

It was the most difficult. When I had cut it down it was incomprehensible and so I just excised it altogether. I don't want to produce something hermetic, something which is inaccessible to the public, because the public is not external to the film, it is internal to it, like rhyme. What decided me was Totò. In the episode he is a petit bourgeois who teaches an eagle how to become a petit bourgeois but ends up becoming an eagle himself: the rationalist, conformist, educated petit bourgeois ends up caught by the eagle and flying away – i.e. religion wins out over conformism and education. But this didn't work because Totò is not a petit bourgeois. His real personality came through and so there was something wrong about the whole episode, although superficially it may have looked all right. Totò just was not a petit bourgeois who would go round and teach good manners to other people.

I found this is a very difficult film indeed, not comic at all, though ideological and sad.

That's a personal impression. I agree it is not very funny, it makes you think more than laugh. But when it was put on in Montreal and New York the audiences laughed a lot, to my great astonishment, unlike in Italy, where they were a bit disappointed, mainly because they went to see Totò and have their usual laugh, which they gradually realized they weren't going to be able to do. Your reaction may be a bit subjective, though I agree it is not a funny film.

Do you ever have a sneak preview?

They do exist, but I've never had one. They sometimes do it for commercial films – they put them on in towns which are supposed to represent the lowest common denominator of potential audiences. The only time I ever see one of my films with an audience is at a festival – *Oedipus*, for example, I saw complete for the first time at Venice. I've never dared to go in and watch one of my films in a normal showing in a public cinema.

I'd like to go back to what you said before about neo-realism. There are two problems. One is about Rossellini: the films he made under fascism are stylistically the same as those he made during the so-called neo-realist period and the same as his later movies, right up to La Prise de Pouvoir par Louis XIV, *which is neo-realist in the sense that* Francesco *is. For me Rossellini is a great – and homogeneous – director. The other problem is the whole categorization of a period as 'neo-realist', lumping together two people like Fellini and Rossellini whom I simply can't consider on the same level, and that would go for almost everybody I know in England. I can see that* Uccellacci e Uccellini *is about aspects of Italian cinema, but I would like to understand more precisely your attitude to Rossellini and neo-realism.*

The stylistic history of Rossellini is the stylistic history of Rossellini, and as I have said before there is a certain fatality in a person's style. Rossellini has a consistent stylistic history, but it is not co-extensive with the history of neo-realism: part of his history coincides with part of neo-realism. The part of Rossellini that coincides with neo-realism has some features in common with Fellini: a certain way of seeing things and people, the way they are shot and the montage are different from the classical cinema which preceded both Fellini and Rossellini. Obviously Fellini and Rossellini are two absolutely different personalities, but the period each of them has in common with neo-realism gives them something in common with each other. The bit of *Uccellacci e Uccellini* you've just mentioned which evokes neo-realism, evokes something typical of both part of Rossellini and part of Fellini: the acrobats, the kind of woman – all that is fairly Fellinian, but it is also Rossellinian. Also they both share what I call 'creatural realism' [*realismo creaturale*], which is a feature of neo-realism typical of a film like *Francesco, Giullare di Dio*: a humble person viewed in a somewhat comic way, piety mixed with irony. I think they both have that. But on the whole I agree with you, they are two directors who have nothing to do with each other, but they both chronologically share a common cultural period which coincides with neo-realism.

So when the crow says 'The age of Brecht and Rossellini is finished' he didn't mean Rossellini is finished, just neo-realism.

Yes, Rossellini was the master of neo-realism and neo-realism is finished. I meant that the age of social denunciation and great ideological drama of the Brecht kind on the one hand and the day-to-day denunciation of the neo-realist kind on the other are both finished.

One of the Italian critics defined your film as the first realist film in Italy. I think Uccellacci e Uccellini *is a realist film, but in very much the same way as, say,* Francesco *could be called realist – in fact all the part of* Uccellacci *with the monks draws heavily on Rossellini's film.*

I love Rossellini, and I love him above all for *Francesco*, which is his finest film. Realism is such an ambiguous and loaded word that it is hard to agree on its meaning. I consider my own films realist compared with neo-realist films. In neo-realist films day-to-day reality is seen from a crepuscular, intimistic, credulous and above all naturalistic point of view. Not naturalistic in the classic sense – cruel, violent and poetic as in Verga, or total as in Zola; in neo-realism things are described with a certain detachment, with human warmth mixed with irony – characteristics which I do not have. Compared with neo-realism I think I have introduced a certain realism, but it would be rather hard to define it exactly.

You said that 'ideological irony' would be useful for analysing Uccellacci e Uccellini: *was this more to do with the condition of the Italian cinema or with the condition of ideology and politics?*

Both. In England or France or America people do not remember the industrial revolution and the transition to prosperity. In Italy this transition has just taken place. What took a century in England has virtually happened in twenty years here. This explosion produced an ideological crisis which particularly threatened the position of marxism, and coinciding with this there was a big cultural change here as well. That is what I was referring to.

NOTES
1. Rossellini has written a text praising *Uccellacci e Uccellini* enthusiastically, which has been used to form a multi-lingual publicity folder.
2. There is actual newsreel of Togliatti's funeral cut into the film.
3. The original scenario and stills from the unused first part are in the volume of *Uccellacci e Uccellini*.

8: La Terra vista dalla Luna and Che Cosa Sono le Nuvole?

La Terra *is part of another sketch film,* Le Streghe: *was there any co-ordination?*

No, everyone worked on his own. I think the rest was finished by the time De Laurentiis asked me to do an episode. Anyway I decided not to look at them, because I might have become demoralized if I'd seen them and anyway I just wanted to fulfil my own project, of which this episode and *Che Cosa Sono le Nuvole?* (my episode in *Capriccio all'Italiana*) are all there is. What I wanted to do originally was make a series of episodes which would make up a full-length feature, all with Totò. When Totò died the idea collapsed. I have vaguely contemplated getting somebody else – I thought of asking Jacques Tati – but now I have rather lost enthusiasm. Anyway, the point is my sketch has nothing to do with the others. The only element of unity is that Silvana Mangano is in all the episodes. The film is a producer's creation not an author's.

Could you at least arrange where your episode appears – because what an audience sees before and afterwards has a huge effect?

Unfortunately, you are quite right. Working on the montage of my own films I've realized that even one image has a huge importance: sometimes if you just take out one frame, which might

La Terra vista dalla Luna: Totò and Ninetto Davoli

seem nothing, it can completely transform a whole scene. All the other episodes in *Le Streghe* are rather alike, they are all basically anachronistic products of neo-realism; even Visconti turned out something fairly poor. All the other episodes are set in a bourgeois milieu and have a brilliant or comic style, so my episode is unassimilable: when it has appeared audiences have just been disconcerted. The same goes for the critics – I don't think any of them have yet said anything sensible about it; they have treated it as though it were simply a kind of bizarre parenthesis in my work, whereas I consider it one of the most successful things I have ever made.

It was a much better vehicle for Totò than Uccellacci e Uccellini.

What happened was that when I'd finished *Uccellacci e Uccellini* I realized that the ideology played a much greater part in it than I had expected: the ideology was not all absorbed by the story, it had not become transformed into poetry, lightness and grace. When I first saw the finished film I felt the ideology was a bit heavy, and so I began to regret that I had not made a much lighter and more fabulous film, even a picaresque film which might have been less meaningful ideologically but which would have been more ambiguous and mysterious, more poetic. I really felt quite sorry about it because Totò and Ninetto were such a lovely couple, and so poetic *per se*; I felt they were full of possibilities. So I thought of making a film which would be all fables, and one of these was *La Terra vista dalla Luna*.

It is basically a surrealist film, as you have said yourself. How do you think surrealism can be reintegrated into cinema (or cinema into surrealism), and why have left-wing critics and the left in general never been very enthusiastic about surrealism?

Well, first, I don't think surrealism is a very clearly defined category. If you think a moment, when we say surrealism we really mean two things – on the one hand we think of the Surrealist Manifesto, of Breton and Aragon, there is the whole group of French surrealists and surrealist painting such as Dali, say, as well as the surrealists at the beginning of the century. And then there is Kafka, who is quite another matter. There is no comparison between Aragon and Eluard or their predecessor Lautréamont, and Kafka, or between surrealist painting and the early surrealist cinema. So, on the one hand there is surrealism as a French cultural and ideological movement in the inter-war period: this was of enormous importance, and I would even go so far as to say that all live contemporary poetry, including that produced by socialist and communist poets comes from this source. It was surrealism that produced the poetry of the Resistance, for example, and even the later 'committed' poetry has a vaguely surrealist origin, though naturally much transformed. Whereas symbolism, which was a contemporary movement, produced all the subsequent reactionary poetry – some of it perhaps very beautiful, but reactionary none the less. The whole of Italian hermeticism and the neo-*avant-garde* have symbolist origins. In this sense the left has, as always, made a mistake. It has been slow to assess or to reassess cultural movements such as these. But my film is anyway not in this tradition: if anything it is rather in the tradition of Kafka's surrealism, or very slightly related to some surrealist painting. It has nothing to do with the surrealism of Buñuel in *Le Chien Andalou*; rather, if anything, it relates to the light, mysterious surrealism of *Belle de Jour*. So the surrealism in my film has rather little relationship to historical surrealism, it is basically the surrealism of fables: its origins are almost popular and it is no accident that the moral of the film 'to be dead or alive is the same thing' is taken from Indian philosophy – it is a kind of slogan of Indian philosophy. The sense of mystery which transforms the landscape and the characters in it into an atmosphere which is not realistic (which we call 'surrealist') is projected by a basically philosophical message, which admittedly comes to me secondhand.

Surrealism is very much a neglected category, particularly in the American cinema. Douglas Sirk, for example, I consider to be a major surrealist.

Buster Keaton has powerful surrealist elements in him. But if you are going to say that, you must make a distinction between historical surrealism (which emerged in France at the beginning of the century), surrealism in painting and the cinema which is quite different again, and what might be called 'meta-historical' surrealism – the surrealism of fables, which you find in La Fontaine, indeed in all the folk-tales of every people; and this has its equivalent in painting, in icons and in folk art. In a certain sense my film comes into this category of meta-historical surrealism.

What did you do about the colours here – did you invent them all?

No, I was very lucky. I found two or three locations which had completely fabulous colours and I just used them. Everything is

La Terra vista dalla Luna: Ninetto Davoli, Silvana Mangano, Totò, and the miracle; *Che Cosa Sono le Nuvole?:* Domenico Modugno takes the puppets to the rubbish dump

real, and the only location that does not come off well is the Colosseum. The others are poor people's seaside resorts, down at Fiumicino and Ostia, where people have built these huts and painted them fantastic colours. The interior of the house where Totò lives and that incredible pink villa with the tower which he climbs to show Silvana Mangano how to pretend to throw herself off the Colosseum are both real.

You did modify the characters though?

Yes, I did have to manipulate them to make them more fabulous. But basically I only accentuated the things I mentioned when I was talking about *Uccellacci e Uccellini*. Totò is such a human person, he is so credulous, so ordinary, so recognizable and so clownesque, all I did was just to emphasize the clownesque in him; and the same with Ninetto – there is something magical in Ninetto, and so I just emphasized this feature. That is all I did, I just emphasized characteristics which were already there, I didn't invent anything.

You can't have endeared yourself to the people connected with the film by making the star deaf and dumb – and in a way it is something of a gesture against the modern cinema as well.

Yes, it is; but the model could only be Chaplin's early comic movies, which were silent. At one point when Silvana Mangano is cleaning out that pile of incredible junk in Totò's house she finds a photograph of Chaplin – that's the key quotation, obviously.

You made Che Cosa Sono le Nuvole? *before* Oedipus?

Yes, I shot it when I came back from looking for locations for *Edipo* in Morocco. I shot it in a week, because I was in a hurry.

There's no connection with the other sketches?

Che Cosa Sono le Nuvole?: Franco Franchi mobbed by a subproletarian audience;
Ninetto Davoli (Othello) and Laura Betti (Desdemona) as human puppets

No, none at all. I'm not even sure what the rest of the film is. My episode was supposed to be part of the famous film I've told you about before; isolated in this other film it will be almost incomprehensible because there will hardly be time for the audience to get the spirit of it; so you should try and imagine it together with the sketch in *Le Streghe* and the other episodes that I never managed to make.

The other day you said you cut a bit which might explain the end better (i.e. to show that the 'puppets' had never been outside): are you thinking of changing the version I saw?

It's too late now because the film's been printed.

You've used Franco Franchi and Ciccio Ingrassia in this episode. These are two very famous comics in Italy, who are known for their own special style. So you're using them two ways – not merely for what they actually are, but also for what they are known to be.

I don't think it's a problem because they are what they are whether they are known to be that or not. I chose them because of their plebeian quality, which is a bit vulgar, like *avanspettacolo*,[1] or popular puppet theatre: their comicness is a bit abject, maybe, but it's also immediate. In Italy people know about their being funny, abroad it will be unknown, but it's still the same thing.

NOTE

1. *Avanspettacolo* is the entertainment which sometimes (increasingly rarely) comes on before the actual film – comics, dancing girls, etc. This can still be found in a few cinemas in the big cities.

9: Oedipus Rex and Amore e Rabbia

There are two initial questions I'd like to ask you about Oedipus. *The first is about Sophocles' text. This is the only case apart from* The Gospel *where you could be said to be working with someone else's script – did you keep to it verbally (because you obviously didn't structurally) as close as you did to Matthew's text? The second is about your interpretation of the Oedipus myth, which is a basically anti-Freudian one; you've given a lot more emphasis to the parricide than to the incest. The myth is an amalgam anyway, so it's an interesting approach because the two things are fairly separate.*

I'm not very well prepared to answer this, because I've really never thought about it. I think the two things are complementary – incest is not possible with the mother unless there's parricide as well. If I remember right, the two have an equal importance in Sophocles' text. You've just pointed out that in my film the parricide comes out more than the incest, certainly emotively if not quantitatively, but I think this is fairly natural because historically I have put myself in a relationship of rivalry and hatred towards my father, so I am freer in the way I represent my relationship towards him, whereas my love for my mother has remained something latent. Even if I understand it rationally, it is difficult to accept it in all its fullness. Perhaps I was inhibited in representing it artistically while I let myself go in the way I represented the parricide. This must be due quite simply to

Freudian reasons, presumably. I hadn't realized it before; but you're right.

In the Prologue you made a very deliberate choice of having a scene where the father says to the baby: 'You're stealing my wife's love.' This is a bit outside the usual Freudian concept of the myth. In fact you're setting up good reasons for the baby to hate his father.

I wanted to make the film freely. When I made it I had two objectives: first, to make a kind of completely metaphoric – and therefore mythicized – autobiography; and second to confront both the problem of psycho-analysis and the problem of the myth. But instead of projecting the myth on to psycho-analysis, I have re-projected psycho-analysis on the myth. This was the fundamental operation in *Oedipus*. But I kept very free, I followed up all my aspirations and impulses. I didn't deny myself a single one. Now, the father's resentment towards his son is something I felt more distinctly than the relationship between the son and the mother, because the relationship between a son and his mother is not a historical relationship, it is a purely interior, private relationship, which is outside history, indeed is meta-historical, and therefore ideologically unproductive, whereas what produces history is the relationship of hatred and love between father and son, so naturally this interested me more than the one between son and mother. I have felt my love for my mother very, very deeply, and all my work is influenced by this, but it is an influence whose origin is deep down inside me and, as I said, rather outside history. While everything ideological, voluntary, active and practical in my actions as a writer depends on my struggle with my father. That's why I put in things which weren't in Sophocles, but which I don't think are outside psycho-analysis, because psycho-analysis talks about the super-ego represented by the father repressing the child; so in a way I just applied psycho-analytic notions in the way I felt.

There are two immediate problems about filming the myth the way you did. One is that the myth is collective; it is the summation of a

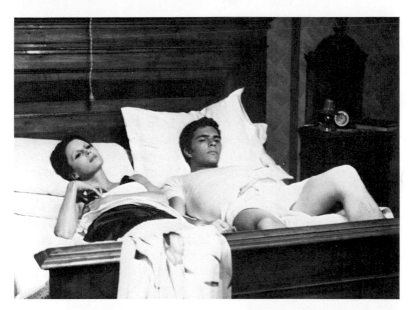

Oedipus Rex: the prologue, parents in bed; Oedipus with his mother (Franco Citti and Silvana Mangano)

collective reaction to certain problems. The second is that these problems were historical problems, problems with a precise location in history, such as the transition from a matriarchal to a patriarchal society. You've put it outside history, very explicitly. I found there was a tension between the Prologue, which is personal (which is the best part of the film), and the part in Morocco which is an attempt to portray a collective myth through an individual. Perhaps this is because the Prologue is an attempt to represent just your own Oedipus complex, but it's more difficult to make a film about the collective myth because no one person actually has the whole 'Oedipus complex'. I found this a bit of a jump.

I think the reason for that is that the beginning is the most inspired part of the film, because it is a fairly particular evocation of my early childhood; it is not an emotional evocation, it is strictly functional and synthetic, so this forced me to be lyrical, as one always has to be with memory, but at the same time to keep very tight control of the material. I think the Prologue in *Oedipus* is one of the best things I have ever done. Obviously the evocation of the myth is less inspired and more deliberate. I wanted to re-create the myth under the aspect of a dream: I wanted all the central part of the film (which is almost the whole movie) to be a kind of dream, and this explains the choice of costumes and settings, the general rhythm of the work. I wanted it to be a kind of aestheticizing dream. Maybe the middle part isn't so good, but I don't think it's because we don't all have the whole myth in us. I wanted to represent the myth like a dream, and I could only present this dream by aestheticizing it; and perhaps this is what is disturbing.

Surely another problem about tackling the Oedipus question through Sophocles is that the causes of neurosis are represented by a god or gods. Everything in Sophocles is outside human control – the family only want to get rid of Oedipus because the gods have told them there'll be trouble if they don't. In the Sophocles text remote causes get pushed out of human range and the whole thing becomes an uncontrollable tragedy.

Oedipus Rex: Franco Citti fighting (ignorance at work); and returning from Delphi

This is exactly what I tried to emphasize, because that is what I liked most in Sophocles, the fact that the person who has to encounter all these problems should be the person most unprepared for all this, someone who is completely innocent. People in Italy criticized me for not making Oedipus an intellectual, because everyone in Italy imagines Oedipus as an intellectual, but I think that is a mistake because an intellectual's vocation is to seek things out; as soon as an intellectual sees something that doesn't work, by vocation he begins to look into it. Whereas Oedipus is exactly the opposite: he is the person who does not want to look into things, like all innocent people, those who live their lives as the prey of life and of their own emotions. That is the thing in Sophocles that inspired me the most: the contrast between total innocence and the obligation to know. It wasn't so much the cruelty of life that produces crimes, but the fact that these crimes are done because people don't try to understand history, life and reality.

But understanding doesn't help either. He does go off and talk to Francesco Leonetti, but even when he knows what's happened he's still back exactly where he was before. That's pretty pessimistic.

Yes, the film is very pessimistic. By the time Oedipus gets to understand it's no use to him. Certainly, one could always play with the hypothesis that if Oedipus had not been so fatally innocent and unconscious, if he had been an intellectual and had first sought out the truth he might have been able to alter reality. The only hope is a cultural one, to be an intellectual. As for the rest I am consistently pessimistic.

It is something that comes up quite a lot in your films; for example, the end of Comizi d'Amore *is based on the antithesis between consciousness and unawareness: the poem you read there is a plea for consciousness, but in general the impression is that you don't think it helps very much. If you're done you're done.*

Oedipus Rex: Franco Citti at Delphi

Well, that's always in me. But I also have a rational tendency in me to be paraenetic towards consciousness and rationality and knowledge, precisely because I am basically irrational and innocent like Oedipus and, at bottom, ignorant. As a reaction I concoct these endorsements of consciousness.

What about where Oedipus says 'Now all is clear, willed, it is not destiny' – at a point where it seems that everything is indeed destiny, and not willed at all?

That is an absolutely mysterious phrase, which I have never been able to understand; but it is in Sophocles. The exact phrase is: 'There, now all is clear, willed, not imposed by destiny.' I cannot understand the phrase, but I find it wonderful, precisely because it is enigmatic and incomprehensible. There is a subtlety underneath which is hard to explain. There is something very clear in the phrase, I feel it could be explained, but I can't do it. Anyway, it's a verse from Sophocles which I lifted just as it stands.

In general, did you leave Sophocles' text much as it was? You added one or two things like the Sphinx, didn't you?

There is a whole background to the story which is told inside the tragedy, which the audience would have known about. In the film this part is almost silent; there is just the odd phrase which I invented like for the Sphinx episode and one or two other things. Basically it is silent. Then there is the second part, the real action which is in Sophocles' *Oedipus*, after the plague and Creon's arrival, and there I have followed Sophocles' text faithfully.

That's your own translation?

Yes, I did a special translation, which is very straightforward and faithful to the original.

What about the music?

That is Rumanian folk-music. Initially I thought of shooting *Oedipus* in Rumania, so I did a trip there to look for locations. But it was not suitable; Rumania is a modern country; the countryside is in the middle of an industrial revolution; all the old wood villages are being destroyed, there's nothing old left. So I gave up the idea of doing it there, but in recompense I found some folk-tunes which I liked a lot because they are extremely ambiguous: they are half-way between Slav, Greek and Arab songs, they are indefinable: it is unlikely that anyone who didn't have specialized knowledge could locate them; they are a bit outside history. As I wanted to make *Oedipus* a myth, I wanted music which was a-historical, a-temporal.

But there's some Japanese music in there, too.

Yes, there is one bit of Japanese music, chosen for the same reason.

Can you explain why you wanted to put it outside history – a-historical – given the two points raised earlier: that you yourself are in history and the myth also belongs to history?

Well, the myth is a product, so to speak, of human history; but then having become a myth it has become absolute, it is no longer typical of this or that period of history, it's typical, let's say, of all history. Perhaps I was wrong to say it is a-historic, it is meta-historical.

There were two scenes that seemed to be shot in a peculiar way: one was when Oedipus visits the Oracle at Delphi, and then the scene at Bologna at the end – did you use special lenses for these?

Not for the scene at Delphi, no. I shot that with normal lenses. The oddness there probably comes from the montage, because I shot the same thing part of the time with Oedipus by himself and part of the time with the crowd and put the two together – perhaps that's what gives the sense of strangeness there is in the Oracle scene. For the last part in the modern age, I used distorting wide-angled lenses because coming back suddenly to the modern world could not be done naturalistically, the transition would have been too brusque; the physical distortion made the transition from meta-history to contemporary history less brusque, it helped to maintain the dream atmosphere.

Why do you think it would have been too brusque otherwise, given that the cinema is both dream and reality already?

Well, it is still brusque anyway: the audience is shocked by the transition. But I didn't mean brusque in the sense of content, I meant it in the formal sense. I had to find some stylistic attenuation.

Oedipus Rex: the plague; sublimation in Bologna (Franco Citti and Ninetto Davoli)

In the Epilogue there are two kinds of music connected with themes that are known in Italy: one tune is connected with the left and the other with the bourgeoisie, is that right?

The Epilogue is what Freud calls the 'sublimation'. Once Oedipus has blinded himself he re-enters society by sublimating all his faults. One of the forms of sublimation is poetry. He plays the pipe, which means, metaphorically, he is a poet. First he plays for the bourgeoisie, and he plays the old Japanese music connected with the Oracle – ancestral, private, confessional music, music that could be defined in one word as decadent: this is a kind of evocation of the primitive, of his origins; then, disgusted by the bourgeoisie, he goes off and plays his pipe (i.e. goes off and acts as a poet) to the workers, and there he plays a tune which was one of the songs of the Resistance: it was a Russian folk-tune which some Italian soldiers learnt in Russia and was sung during the Resistance as a revolutionary song.

When you were talking about Orgia *[see pages 140–1] the other day, you said the only words in the film would be when somebody says what enormous pleasure he got from killing his father. Obviously one of the frustrating things in the Oedipus myth is that everything is unconscious – if someone* wants *to kill his father he might as well at least get pleasure out of it. So would it be right to see* Orgia *as a development of the Oedipus problem in that sense?*

Orgia is not a myth, it is a film with a thesis. The person does everything innocently, but just before he dies he realizes what pleasure he felt doing all these things. In taste, the sensuality of its images, in costumes and faces *Orgia* will probably be more like *The Gospel* than *Oedipus*: it will link up with all my other films, of course, but it will be more a film with a thesis.

You've shot an episode of Vangelo '70[1] *as well.*

Yes, it's called *Il Fico Innocente*, I think. It's very short, only twelve minutes. Initially it was just one long tracking shot all the

Vangelo '70: walking up the Via Nazionale; Pasolini and Ninetto Davoli

way up the Via Nazionale in Rome. It's still twelve minutes long, but I've cut in two or three different shots. *Vangelo '70* is supposed to be inspired by parables or bits in the Gospels, so for my episode I chose the innocent fig tree – you remember where Christ wants to pick some figs but because it's March the tree hasn't produced any figs yet so he curses it. This is an episode which has always been very mysterious to me and there are several contradictory interpretations of it. The way I've interpreted it goes like this: that there are moments in history when one cannot be innocent, one must be aware; not to be aware is to be guilty. So I got Ninetto to walk up Via Nazionale and while he's walking along without a thought in his head and completely innocent a number of images of some of the important and dangerous things happening in the world pass superimposed across the Via Nazionale – things he is not aware of like the Vietnam War, relations between the West and the East and so on: these are just shadows which pass above him which he does not know about. Then at a certain moment you hear the voice of God in the middle of the traffic urging him to know, to be aware, but like the fig tree he does not understand because he is immature and innocent and so at the end God condemns him and makes him die.

NOTE

1. The title of the film was later changed from *Vangelo '70* to *Amore e Rabbia* and the title of Pasolini's sequence in it from *Il Fico Innocente* to *La Fiore di Campo*.

I'd like to ask you a bit about how you work. Totò laid some stress on the fact that you shot everything in very short takes: [1] *is that your normal method?*

Yes, I always shoot very short takes. Referring back to what I said earlier, this is the essential difference between me and the neo-realists. The main feature of neo-realism is the long take; the camera sits in one place and films a scene as it would be in real life, with people coming and going, talking to each other, looking at each other just like they would in real life. Whereas I never use a long take (or virtually never). I hate naturalness. I reconstruct everything. I never have somebody talking in a long shot away from the camera, I have to have him talking straight into the camera, so there is never a scene in any of my films where the camera is to one side and the characters are talking away among themselves. They are always in *champ contre champ*. So I shoot like that – each person says his bit and that's it. I never do a whole scene all in one take.

This must have created difficulties with some actors? Surely some of them must have wanted to know what was happening?

Yes. It works easily with non-professionals, because they do everything I ask them to, and anyway it is easier for them to behave naturally. I must admit professional actors get a bit traumatized because they are used to having to act. Besides – and this is rather important for defining my way of working – real life is full of nuances and actors like to be able to reproduce them. An actor's great ambition is to start out weeping and then move very very gradually through all the different stages of emotion to laughing. I hate nuances and I hate naturalism, so an actor inevitably feels a bit disappointed working with me because I remove some of the basic elements of his craft, indeed *the* basic element – miming naturalness. So for Anna Magnani it was a major crisis to have to work with me. Totò argued a little and then gave in. Silvana Mangano accepted immediately without the slightest discussion, and I think this method suited her, because she is a very fine actress.

You've acted a bit yourself – as the High Priest in Oedipus, *and for Lizzani in* Il Gobbo. *How did that happen?*

I've acted twice for Lizzani. He is an old friend of mine and I just couldn't say no. I quite enjoyed it, and it was quite useful just to give me an idea of what a set was like – because I did the part in *Il Gobbo* before I made *Accattone*. It was a bit of a holiday as well, I did a lot of reading. The other part was in a western he made recently, where I play a Mexican priest on the side of the rebels.[2]

Directors work in different ways in different countries. Do you give all the actors the complete script?

When it exists, yes. But *Theorem*, for example, I shot almost without a script at all. Silvana Mangano saw it for the first time when the film was half finished. But in general I always give the actors the script out of politeness, though in fact I prefer to talk to them about the part. No method is perfect because, as you know very well, if I say 'sad' there are infinite gradations of sadness; if I say 'egoistic' there are plenty of different ways to be egoistic. Basically I prefer to set it up by talking to the actor and trying to define the part like that.

Do you tend to change the script much while you're shooting?

No, in general the only changes are minor adaptations either because of the setting or, more usually, to the character when I see how he or she is working out in the part.

What about Franco Citti in Accattone – *although you did not use his voice at all, did you fix what he was supposed to say with him before shooting?*

Oh yes. The whole script was written for him personally, even though he did not speak it. I wrote every line for him, and the script in the film is exactly as I wrote it, down to the last comma.

What about Orson Welles – was it difficult to direct him? Did the fact that he was both a great director and a great intellectual lead to de facto *co-direction?*

No, no, Welles is both an intellectual and an extremely intelligent person; he was a very obedient actor. I am just the same with Lizzani, I never open my mouth. I think directors understand this better than anybody. It was really wonderful working with Orson Welles, in fact I tried very hard to get him for *Theorem*, but it was impossible, but I'm thinking of trying to get him for *St Paul*.

What about the American cinema? The last time I heard you talking about this you were fairly enthusiastic about Shadows, *and* It's a Mad, Mad, Mad, Mad World, *but you seemed not to be following the American cinema very closely:*[3] *is this still the case?*

I used to go a lot when I was younger, in fact until I started making films; since then I've been going much less. I'm not quite sure why this is. One factor certainly is that after a whole day working at a

Silvana Mangano 'accepted without the slightest hesitation . . . because she is a very fine actress'

film I find it physically impossible to go back to the cinema; after hours and hours in front of a moviola I just don't feel like it. Then I get slightly panic-stricken when confronted with a film which is finished – Fellini doesn't go to the cinema at all now ever and I can understand him, though I think it is a bit much never to go. Also I have become much more demanding: I can't go to a cinema for entertainment any longer, just to enjoy myself at some American movie, I used to like doing that, but now I will only go if I'm guaranteed 90 per cent that the film is going to be good – and that only happens about five or six times a year.

But do you still follow up directors you were interested in before – would you definitely go and see a new Ford, for example?

Well, Ford is a bad example, because I don't much like him. I don't like the great epic American directors. I did like the American cinema very much when I was younger but I don't like it now, though there are still some directors I would go and see if they made a new film. I don't feel I have got very much from the American cinema except the myth of the cinema which I'll leave to Godard and the *Cahiers du Cinéma*. Basically the real myth of the cinema came to me from the authors I mentioned earlier, from the silent cinema.

When you went, whom did you follow?

Well, it was all a bit indistinct then, I just went to see average American products; I think most of the directors I liked weren't really American anyway, they were Europeans who had emigrated to America – people like Lang and Lubitsch – but I didn't like the last big American productions just before the war, or the post-war stuff – say, people like Kazan. I can sometimes admire them, but I don't like them.

You have mentioned the importance to you of Mizoguchi: do you follow the Japanese cinema as a whole?

Very few Japanese films come to Italy, unfortunately. I don't like Kurosawa nearly as much, but I like what I've seen of Kon Ichikawa – *The Burmese Harp* was a very fine film, so was the film on the Olympics.

What about the general condition of the Italian cinema? In Uccellacci e Uccellini *you portray the death of neo-realism, but can you see anything to take its place, or just chaos? Is there anybody here you follow particularly?*

The situation as I see it is extremely simple: Italian neo-realism moved into France and England. It has not finished. The only place it is dead is in Italy. It has changed its nature and become a different cultural entity, but it has continued in France with Godard and in the new English cinema, which I don't like at all (though I do like Godard). The odd thing is that after moving into France and England particularly via the myth of Rossellini, neo-realism is appearing again in Italy with the younger directors: Bertolucci and Bellocchio are carrying on Italian neo-realism filtered back via Godard and the English cinema.

One of the most surprising things about coming to Italy is that a lot of cinéphiles *here are very enthusiastic about all the English directors I can't stand. Do you think this is a devious cultural response to the neo-realist influence?*

I think so. Even without doing a breakdown on a moviola I think you can see the English cinema is very much influenced by neo-realism. I was in England just a while ago and I saw half of *Poor Cow* – even a child could see it is a product of Italian neo-realism which has moved into a different context.

Bertolucci of course started out as your assistant on Accattone.

Yes. Then later he made *La Commare Secca*, which I was originally going to do. When I made *Accattone* he knew nothing about the cinema at all; but then I have always avoided having professional assistants. Sometimes this can be a disadvantage, but I much prefer to work with someone who understands me and can give me moral support than to work with a professional. Recently, I've just started in the theatre, and my first demand to the financial backers has been that I should not have to be subjected to the stench of the theatre world, that there should be no professional assistants around.

If Bertolucci is one of the directors bringing neo-realism back into Italian cinema, how do you assess your influence on him?

I think more than being influenced by me, he reacted against me. I was rather like a father to him, and so he reacted against me. In fact when he was shooting a scene he would think to himself 'How would Pier Paolo shoot this?' and so he would decide to shoot it a different way. Maybe I gave him something indefinable, but he was always able to tell the authentic from the inauthentic. I only had a very general influence on him, and as regards style he is completely different from me. His real master is Godard.

As you write, direct, choose the music, locations and almost everything else for your films, there is not very much to ask you about the people you work with, but could you say something about Alfredo Bini and Sergio Citti?

Bini had confidence in me at a time when that was extremely hard: I knew nothing about the cinema, and he gave me *carte blanche* and let me work in peace. Sergio Citti has indeed been a very valuable collaborator, first on the dialogue of the novels and now on the movie scripts. I find it very easy to work with him, and he is extremely proficient at everything now.

All your editing is done by Nino Baragli, who seems to be your most permanent colleague.

Yes, this is the one case where I trust a professional. Baragli is a very practical person. He has made thousands of films. He is full of good sense, and he is a Roman, so he has a sense of irony, so I use him to keep a rein on some of my excesses. He is the voice of common sense. But even here I never let him do anything on his own. We always work together on the moviola and he just does the technical side of it, putting the bits together.

In previous interviews you've talked about two projects: one was Il Padre Selvaggio *and the other was supposed to be about a saint like St Francis. I know that* Il Padre Selvaggio *was interrupted by the case over* La Ricotta – *but what happened to the other project?*

Yes, *Il Padre Selvaggio* only got as far as a scenario. The other project I had at the time was called *Bestemmia* which I gave up because I did *The Gospel*. But I've gone on working on it and I've written it out as a poem – it's a script in verse form. Eventually I'll publish it as I've been dragging it round now for five or six years.[4]

That wasn't going to be the film about a character like Charles de Foucauld?

No, Charles de Foucauld was another vague project. I've decided to scrap that idea and all the other saint ideas I have had and do a life of Paul, which I'm going to start in the spring of 1969. It will be completely transported into modern times: New York will be Rome, Paris will be Jerusalem and Rome will be Athens. I've tried to find a series of analogies between the capitals of the world today and the capitals of the ancient world, and I've done the same thing for the actual events – e.g. the opening episode where Paul who is a Pharisee, a collaborator and a reactionary, is standing by at the murder of St Stephen, along with the executioners, is going to be done in the film with an analogous episode during the Nazi occupation of Paris, where Paul will be a reactionary Parisian collaborator who kills a Resistance fighter. The whole film's going to be transpositions like that. But I'm going to be extremely faithful to the text of St Paul and his words will be exactly the words he uses in his letters.

But that's not what you're going to do when you've finished Theorem?

No, the project I had, which I have got the financing for, is called *Notes for a Poem on the Third World*, which would be shot in Africa, India, the Arab countries, Latin America and the black ghettoes in North America; in each place there would be a complete episode, half documentary and half location reconnaissance for a future film: it would be told indirectly, like a story to be told. That was the idea. But just in the last week I have changed my mind because I realized that the film would have no audience. As I have said before, the public is inside a film. But if I made a film on the third world, it is obvious that I would aim it at the élites. It would be an essay, not a narrative film, because I am not a vulgarizer. The only way I would get a mass audience would be by adapting my work to the level of the *Reader's Digest* which I would never do. As you know, third world audiences are conditioned to Indian epics and Sophia Loren. Then there is another thing: the film would be very polemical towards both marxism and the student movement. I'm not going to make the film yet. I shall make it bit by bit, because it is something I very much want to do.

Instead I have decided to make a normal film, in two parts: the first will be called *Orgy* [*Orgia*] and the second *Pigsty* [*Porcile*]. The *Orgy* episode is something I wrote about three years ago, after the producer of Buñuel's *Simeon del Desierto* came to Europe to see if he could find a second episode to put alongside the Buñuel (which is a stupendous film, perhaps Buñuel's finest). So I fixed up the episode, and it's been sitting in a drawer ever since, but every now and then I get a great urge to make it into a film. Very briefly, it is about a man at some imprecise date in history, the Middle Ages or something like that, who is dying of hunger in the middle of the desert, just eating bits of grass and mud so that he is reduced to the condition of a monster, virtually. One day he comes across a place in the desert where there has been a battle

Collaborators: Alfredo Bini, Sergio Citti and Orson Welles on the set of *La Ricotta*

and there are a whole lot of dead soldiers lying round in their armour. So he steals the armour off one of them and puts it on and in this way he feels sufficiently confident to move off to the edge of the desert where one day some other soldiers pass by. One of these falls behind a bit and this other character attacks him. There is a long fight, because they are both young, and eventually the famished one from the desert wins. He remains seated a long time on the corpse of the other soldier, until he gets the idea of eating him, which he does after cutting off his head and throwing it into a chasm. Gradually other bandits appear round him and they form a little band, all affected with the vice of cannibalism. They live for a while attacking passers-by in the desert until one day one of them manages to escape to the nearest town where there is some feudal ruler who then captures the whole band. All of them are burnt alive except for him. He is put through a brief trial, which he can't hear, and then buried alive. His last words, which are also the only words in the film because the whole thing is silent, are about the incomparable pleasure he felt killing his father and eating human flesh.

The second episode is called *Pigsty*, which is the name of the whole film [*Porcile*]. This takes place in the industrialized part of Germany, at Godesberg, near Cologne, which is where Adenauer used to live, in the villa of a big German industrialist rather like Krupp, say – one of the old industrial families. This industrialist has a mysterious son. A girl is in love with the son, but the son does not reciprocate her love, although he is not in love with anybody else. He says he wants to take part in the student movement and then he doesn't. He is 50 per cent with the conformists and 50 per cent with the non-conformists, so he is nothing. His father has an economic and political rival he is trying to eliminate, and through detectives he has found out that his rival was a Nazi criminal with a collection of Jewish skeletons. He is just about to eliminate him when the rival turns up at his house and tells him about his own son, because the rival had had the same idea of destroying his competitor, and so he'd done some spying on him as well. This had revealed that the mysterious son could only have erotic relations with pigs, hence his frequent visits to the sty. So the two industrialists, the neo-capitalist with the Nazi past and the more cultured paleo-capitalist unite and do a merger. Just at this moment the son goes off as usual to the pigsty and sees Spinoza in a vision. Spinoza explains his life to him and tells him that his love for the pigs is equivalent to an affirmation of the existence of God and leaves him. This is right in the middle of the merger celebrations. Some farmers appear and tell the old industrialist that the young man has been eaten by the pigs. The old man listens carefully, and when he has satisfied himself that there is absolutely nothing left, not even a button or anything like that, he says to the farmers: 'All right, don't say anything about this to anybody', and that's the end.

Recently you have also become very interested in the theatre, evidenced by your 'Manifesto for a new Theatre'.[5] As far as I'm concerned,

*the theatre is dead, so I'm quite curious to know why you have become
so interested in it. I realize you want to destroy the theatre as it is,
but all the same it doesn't seem to me a tradition within which any
renovation can be done.*

It's a bit difficult to answer, because I got interested in the theatre
and wrote that 'Manifesto' simply because I wrote some texts for
the theatre, but I don't know why I wrote them in the first place.
Some time ago I was in bed for about a month with an ulcer and
I just picked up a pen and the first thing I wrote were these plays
in verse. The point is that I had not written any poetry for several
years, and then suddenly I started again, but for the theatre, and
in fact I've never written with such ease as I have done for the
theatre, and nothing has ever been such fun. That's just the texts,
of course, I don't know about the staging. Maybe it was partly
because when I was ill I read Plato's *Dialogues* and I was absolutely
bowled over by how beautiful they were. In fact one of the films
I might make, which would be my last film, after *St Paul* and after
another called *Calderón*, which is still only in the project stage,
would be a life of Socrates. I know this is an old project of Rossellini's, but as he won't make up his mind to do it, I will.

So anyway, I wrote these six tragedies, which forced me to
think about the theatre and how they might be put on. Up to then
I thought the way you do, that the theatre is dead. Normally I
would not have bothered to give my text to anyone because I'm
not interested in having them put on the way they would normally
be in Italy – at least in England there is not the problem of the
language, the actors speak decently. But the fact that I had six
tragedies sitting on my desk forced me to adopt a position and
formulate my theories in this manifesto.

Pilade is the only one I've seen published: did it have much resonance?[6]

Absolutely none. I might as well have published a hundred blank
pages for all the echo it had – which tends to confirm what you
were saying, but I feel it also confirms what I said in the

'Manifesto': that the theatre is dead because the people in it have no interest in culture. *Pilade* is the only one that has been published so far, but all the others are ready and I think I'll bring them out as a volume under the title *Porcile*, because the story I told you about the film project is one of these.

Why do you say the life of Socrates would be your last film?

Well, I've said that before. It's hard to know what to say. I would like my last film to be about Socrates, but let's hope that something will come up between *St Paul* and *Socrates*. To do a film on Socrates I will have to reach a stage where I have completely exhausted all the marginal motives which push me to make movies, and arrive at a totally disinterested cinema, one which is completely pure: like I did in part with *Uccellacci e Uccelini*, but only in very small part; I would like to achieve greater purity and greater disinterestedness; I would like a purer relationship with the audience. So a life of Socrates would be ideally my ultimate film – I would like it to be the culmination of my cinema experience.

NOTES

1. Interview for Italian TV, in *Cahiers du Cinéma* 192.
2. *Requiescant.*
3. Interview in *Filmcritica* 156–7 (April–May, 1965).
4. The scenario of *Il Padre Selvaggio* can be found in *Cinema e Film* 3 and 4. There is a fragment of *Bestemmia* in *Cinema e Film* 2.
5. 'Manifesto per un nuovo teatro', *Nuovi Argomenti* 9 (nuova serie).
6. 'Pilade', *Nuovi Argomenti* 7–8 (nuova serie).

11: Cinema and Theory

Your project Porcile *is a play you've already written. Previously, when asked about making a film of one of your novels[1] you have said that you would not make a film of one of your existing texts because it would be like doing the same thing twice.*

Well, the reason is that my semiological studies have led me to bring the theatre and the cinema very close to each other theoretically. The theatre is only a long take; it has several features in common with the cinema: both represent reality with reality. In both, for example, if I want to represent you, I would do so with yourself, with your body, your expressions, your psychology, your gestures, your education, etc. In both a body is represented by a body, an object by that object. When I write a scene for the theatre in fact this scene is also a movie scene, as I conceive of the theatre, because all I am doing is producing a movie sequence made up of a long take. Whereas transforming a book into a film means remaking a work and therefore mixing up all the profound motives that produced it originally, filming a theatre scene faithfully means performing the same operation – it does not involve mixing up anything, only a minor change of technique.

But in 'La Fine dell' Avanguardia'[2] you maintained that there was a hierarchy: the theatre mimes *reality, but the cinema* reproduces *it.*

Now you seem to have promoted the theatre – and abandoned your previous ideas.

Yes, I have 'promoted' the theatre, as you put it, to the semio-logical level of the cinema. This is since I went deeper into the fact that the cinema is an audio-visual technique; I definitively abandoned the idea of the cinema as an image (which is said rhetorically out of bias, but is ridiculous) – the cinema is not image, it is an audio-visual technique in which the word and the sound have the same importance as the image. Once this is established, highly verbal theatre has, semiologically, the same value as the cinema.

What do you think of Lévi-Strauss's idea that the cinema should be used to film vast theatre scenes which you can't achieve on a stage?[3] Are you interested in that yourself?

No, that's not what I'm after at all. What I have done is to break the convention which said that the theatre and the cinema are two very different things; in fact they are the same, though they may be different techniques: both are systems of signs which coincide with the system of signs of reality. A word spoken by you and followed by a gesture is the same word followed by a gesture that you would produce on a stage or would be captured by a movie camera. In both theatre and the cinema they are linguistic signs whose archetype is in reality.

Surely one of the reasons Pilade *got such a silent reception is that it is very difficult to read a script – not only a theatre script, but any kind; I find it very difficult to* see *a script as a play or a film. I could read* Pilade *as poetry, but not as a play. I think this is fairly common.*

It isn't to me. In 'La sceneggiatura come "struttura che vuol essere altra struttura" '[4] I've written about that. I see both a film script and the written text of a play as structures which tend to become other structures, I read their tension, I follow them in their movement: the opposite happens to me of what happens to you. Even when I read a really awful script I can always see the other structure it wants to become; so obviously it is a factor of individual psychology. I must admit that I can more easily read a script as a future film than I can the text of a play as a future play, because a theatre text is more complete as a literary script, so one is more rooted in the literary structure.

You've accused the Italian neo-avant-garde of reducing the language [lingua] *to zero and therefore values to zero.*[5] *What did you mean by this, and why have you attacked the neo-avant-garde when you've been a member of the* avant-garde *yourself until now?*

I can't remember the exact context in which I made that remark; however, I could clarify it like this. The *avant-garde* has made a historical error. It thought that the Italian language was a *lingua A*, which it criticized. According to them this *lingua A* was purely a language of communication, purely colloquial and practical while at the literary level it was considered traditional, official, etc. So they engaged in a polemic against this *lingua A* by breaking up its schemas: they thought that by reversing a phrase or making a casual collage of words or producing a linguistic scandal with grammatical or syntactical innovations they could have a profound effect – on the content, on the mind of the reader, on his habits, and therefore on his class differentiations and determinations. All this was a mistake, because as I see it, there is no *lingua A* at the present time. All there is is a *lingua A* which is becoming a *lingua B*. Italian is moving. They thought they were shooting at a stationary target, but in fact it was moving. Italian is changing from a dialect-based language, based on Florentine, into a single language guided no longer by a literary language but by the language of technology. The Italian language [*lingua*] is undergoing a revolution of its own. The *avant-garde's* revolution was really only a tiny and mistaken literary revolution while something else much more important was taking place in the language as a whole.

Do you think that the new technological language has won the day in Italy?

Not at all. The phenomenon has appeared, and it is irresistible. It is impossible to pretend it isn't there. But I can't say what stage it has reached, or exactly how it will finish: maybe there will be interruptions in the process, I just can't say. However, logically I think that is our future, and I have scandalized a lot of people in Italy by saying so – the *avant-garde,* and all the left-wing linguists and university professors who had been churning out the old rhetoric about Italian Unity being achieved through the integration of the artificial language based on Florentine, through the integration from below of the popular languages, the contribution of dialects, etc. All this has been proved false. It could have become true if the Communist Party had become a hegemonic party, if Italian culture had developed under the hegemony of the working class, but this didn't happen and so the idea of Unity taking place through an integration of the popular language is an illusory one.

When you were asked what was the relationship between your theories and the films you make, you said that these texts are 'observations of a grammatical character which have nothing to do with my work as a writer: it is like asking a writer what a gerund is and then asking him what its place is in his work; I have not written as an aesthetician, I have spoken as a linguist'.[6] Is there any relationship, because it would seem there must be, particularly as you have entitled one of your texts 'Appunti en poète per una linguistica marxista'?[7]

The *en poète* simply means that they are done as a dilettante. My theories are at a linguistic level: it is impossible to fix a relationship between a grammarian and the poetry he may write, they are two completely different fields. If my theoretical research was on an aesthetic plane you could ask me what relationship there is between aesthetic theory and aesthetic production. But as my theories are on a linguistic and grammatical plane there is a qualitative gap between the two things. However, I should say that I do carry out my theoretical studies on linguistics and grammar *en poète*, as a dilettante, and therefore there is in fact a relationship: in effect it has been my semiological research into the cinema which has explained to me why I make movies.

There is a very striking gap in general between cinema and cinema criticism. As you both make movies and write about cinema theory, could you, for example, produce a theoretical criticism of one of your own movies?

Yes, I think I could. I have in fact done a breakdown of certain films. In one of my texts[8] (which was originally a talk at Pesaro) I've documented my argument with an analysis of some brief sequences of two films, one by Olmi and one by Bertolucci. When I was giving the talk, I put them on a normal screen, but I did the original analysis on a moviola. I did much the same thing with a Ford film on a moviola at the Centro Sperimentale during the student occupation of the school.[9] This wasn't an aesthetic breakdown, it was purely grammatical and syntactical. It was an attempt to establish by close study of the text and not intuitively (naturally with intuition you can understand anything in two words), whether the film in question was written in the language of prose or the language of poetry – i.e. just a first step towards a stylistic examination. With literature all you have to do is open a page to see if the text is in prose or poetry, but with the cinema this is more difficult. But I think my analyses have shown that this can quite easily be done for the cinema, too, which is an essential first step for any more thorough examination. The Ford turned out to be in prose.

In 'The Cinema of Poetry', which is the only text of yours that has been translated into English as far as I know,[10] you introduce the concept of dreamlikeness [oniricità], which has been widely criticized. One of the criticisms is that it obscures the fact that when you make a film you in fact have much more *control over the images used than when you write; you actually choose them yourself, your choice is open, whereas the drift of saying something is dreamlike is to stress the spontaneity and lack of control in the process.*

When I said the cinema is dreamlike, I didn't mean anything very important, it was just something I said like that casually. All I meant was that an image is more dreamlike than a word. Your dreams are cinematographic dreams, they are not literary dreams. Even a sound image, say thunder booming in a clouded sky, is somehow infinitely more mysterious than even the most poetic description a writer could give of it. A writer has to find oniricity through a highly refined linguistic operation, while the cinema is much nearer to sounds physically, it doesn't need any elaboration. All it needs is to produce a clouded sky with thunder and straight away you are close to the mystery and ambiguity of reality.

But dreams are usually very weak in films – Fellini's dream sequences just aren't like dreams at all.

That is simply because the cinema is already a dream. Fellini's films are particularly dreamlike, deliberately: everything is seen as a kind of dream, a kind of surrealistic and dreamlike deformation so, naturally, it is rather difficult to insert a dream into a movie which already has the characteristics of a dream. But take Bergman, who is much less dreamlike, perhaps more mysterious but less obviously dreamlike: the dream in *Wild Strawberries* is remarkable, it comes very close to what dreams are really like.

In the text 'In Calce al "Cinema di Poesia"'[11] you use the word 'kineme' [cinéma] to describe a third operation, the production of an image, which you claim oral and graphic signs produce: this idea has been criticized, particularly as confusing reference [riferimento] and the signified [significato].[12] Do you still stand by the idea?

Whenever I have spoken about kinemes [*cinéma*], I have always done so speculatively and tentatively. When I study the language of cinema as a language [*lingua*], as a system of signs, I always act on the premise that it is wrong to consider written-spoken signs as an archetype or a model: it is useless looking for analogies because there may be systems of signs and communication radically diverse from the written-spoken. So we must broaden the concept of language [*lingua*], just as cybernetics has broadened the concept of life. This has always been my basic premise. So when I have spoken about phonemes I have slightly been contradicting myself by looking for analogies between the cinematographic system of signs and the linguistic system of signs. I used the word 'kinemes' by analogy with the word 'phonemes', which involves a code to try and establish a kind of double articulation in the cinema as in the language [*lingua*]. Martinet maintains that the characteristic of language [*lingua*] is double articulation. I have tried to find something similar in the cinema, but without giving excessive importance to it; it was just a possibility.

You have quite rightly said that there is an enormous increase in interest in the cinema at a moment when the cinema itself is badly on the decline – and you ascribe this to the fact that marxism has become fashionable. I agree with the general proposition, but the explanation won't do for a country like America, will it? Were you just thinking about Italy?

Yes, I think I was mainly concerned with Italy, and Europe – *auteurs'* films. As long as marxism was a living culture, with considerable weight in public life some films by *auteurs* were valorized and thus found a way to be seen and distributed. But when marxism was overtaken by events it fell into a crisis and thus to some extent lacks prestige, and since then films by *auteurs* have found much less support. So clearly it was something which concerned both Italy and Europe.

When you wrote 'Laboratorio' you were very enthusiastic about Hjelmslev because you said that he had managed to introduce the concept of value into structuralism.[13] As you know, Hjelmslev has

Louis Hjelmslev; Roman Jakobson

*been much attacked by the structuralists. Do you still intend to pursue
your research along Hjelmslevian lines, as you did then?*

I disagree strongly with the French structuralists, however much
I admire someone like Lévi-Strauss. And in fact the conclusion of
my article there was to abandon the word 'structure' completely
and use the word 'process' instead, which implies the word 'value'.
A structure evolves inasmuch as there exist values which make it
evolve, values which to some extent are inherent in it, but ensure
that they do not ossify into a kind of old-style French rationalism.
My choice of the word 'process' indicates my disagreement with
structuralism, and the notion of value comes in here.

*In 'The Cinema of Poetry' you mention the importance of making
the audience aware of the camera as a criterion of poetic cinema.
There has been some confusion as to whether you meant that the*

cinema is naturally poetry and if so, first, how prose cinema has managed on the whole to impose itself and, second, if it is naturally poetry in what way does making people aware of the camera determine whether or not it is poetry?

In my view the cinema is substantially and naturally poetic, for the reasons I have stated: because it is dreamlike, because it is close to dreams, because a cinema sequence and a sequence of memory or of a dream – and not only that but things in themselves – are profoundly poetic: a tree photographed is poetic, a human face photographed is poetic because physicity is poetic in itself, because it is an apparition, because it is full of mystery, because it is full of ambiguity, because it is full of polyvalent meaning, because even a tree is a sign of a linguistic system. But who talks through a tree? God, or reality itself. Therefore the tree as a sign puts us in communication with a mysterious speaker. Therefore, the cinema by directly reproducing objects physically, etc., etc., is substantially poetic. This is one aspect of the problem, let's say pre-historic, almost pre-cinematographic. After that we have the cinema as a historical fact, as a means of communication, and as such it too is beginning to develop into different subspecies, like all communications media. Just as literature has a language [*lingua*] for prose and a language [*lingua*] for poetry, so does the cinema. That's what I was saying. In this case you must forget that the cinema is naturally poetic because it is a type of poetry, I repeat, which is pre-historic, amorphous, unnatural. If you see a bit of the most banal western ever made or any old commercial film, if you look at it in a non-conventional way, even a film like that will reveal the dreamlike and poetic quality which there is physically and naturally in the cinema, but this is not the cinema of poetry. The cinema of poetry is the cinema which adopts a particular technique just as a poet adopts a particular technique when he writes verse. If you open a book of poetry, you can see the style immediately, the rhymes and all that: you see the language [*lingua*] as an instrument, or you count the syllables of a verse. The equivalent of what you see in a text of poetry you can also find in a cinema text, through the stylemes, i.e. through the camera movements and the montage. So to make films is to be a poet.

NOTES

1. *Filmcritica* 125. (September 1962) Cf. Pasolini in *Films and Filming*, January 1961.
2. *Nuovi Argomenti* 3–4. Cf. Christian Metz, 'A propos de l'impression de réalité au cinéma', *Cahiers du Cinéma* 166–7; also in *Filmcritica* 163 with an excellent presentation by Adriano Aprà discussing the relationship between the positions of Metz, Pasolini and Rohmer, and relating the current discussion to that which took place in the U.S.S.R. in the early thirties.
3. See interview with Lévi-Strauss, *Cahiers du Cinéma* 156.
4. *Nuovi Argomenti* 1 (nuova serie); now in the volume of *Uccellacci e Uccellini* and in French in *Cahiers du Cinéma* 185.
5. In 'Laboratorio', *Nuovi Argomenti* 1 (nuova serie); 'Appunti *en poète* per una linguistica marxista.'
6. *Filmcritica* 174 (February 1967).
7. 'Appunti *en poète* per una linguistica marxista', *Nuovi Argomenti* 1 (nuova serie).
8. 'La Lingua Scritta dell'Azione', *Nuovi Argomenti* 2 (nuova serie). The two films are *Il tempo si è fermato* (Olmi) and *Prima della Rivoluzione* (Bertolucci).
9. From Pasolini's description, this seemed to be *Gideon of Scotland Yard* (John Ford, 1959).
10. 'The Cinema of Poetry', *Cahiers du Cinéma in English* 6.
11. 'In Calce al "Cinema di Poesia" ', *Filmcritica* 163 (January 1966).
12. In particular by Vittorio Saltini, 'Sulla presunta razionalità del linguaggio filmico', *Nuovi Argomenti* 2 (nuova serie). Cf. Pio Baldelli, 'L'Ideologia nelle strutture del linguaggio', *ibid*. Both these texts were originally papers delivered at the 1966 Pesaro Festival and therefore refer mainly to Pasolini's 1965 intervention.
13. In particular a paper delivered by Hjelmslev in Oslo in 1957.

Appendix: Theorem

Extract from an interview on BBC Television (*Release*)

In Theorem *you show a certain compassion, one might even say sympathy for the bourgeoisie – why is this?*

This is the first film I have shot in a bourgeois milieu with bourgeois characters. Up till now I have never done this because I could not bear to have to live with people I could not stand for months on end, fixing the script and then shooting the film.

But my hatred for the bourgeoisie is really a kind of physical repugnance towards petit bourgeois vulgarity, the vulgarity of hypocritical 'good manners', and so on. And perhaps it is above all because I find their cultural meanness insufferable.

Anyway this time I decided to do a film with Terence Stamp on the bourgeoisie. But I chose people who were not particularly odious, people who elicited a certain human sympathy – they are typical of the bourgeoisie, but not of the worst bourgeoisie. Besides all this, it is only right that I should feel something for all individuals, including bourgeois individuals.

What about the Terence Stamp character? Is he really religious – and who is he really?

I adapted my character to the physical and psychological person of the actor. Originally, I intended this visitor to be a fertility god, the typical god of pre-industrial religion, the sun-god, the Biblical god, God the Father. Naturally, when confronted with things as they were, I had to

Theorem: Terence Stamp with Anne Wiazemsky, and Massimo Girotti's feet

abandon my original idea and so I made Terence Stamp into a generically ultra-terrestrial and metaphysical apparition: he could be the Devil, or a mixture of God and the Devil. The important thing is that he is something authentic and unstoppable.

Why did Theorem *cause such a scandal?*

There are plenty of reasons, which are neither strictly cultural nor cinematographic: the first is probably the fact that it was in the centre of the cyclone which is hitting the Church at the moment, with a clerical left and clerical right and so on. The film won a prize from the left Catholics, and has been violently attacked by the Curia and the conservative wing of the Church. I think this is the main reason.

Extract from an interview with Pasolini by Lino Pèroni, *Inquadrature*, 15-16, Autumn 1968

A number of recent films (such as Uccellaci e Uccellini, I Sovversivi, La Guerre est Finie, La Chinoise) *seem to have a common denominator, in that they all – at different levels, and with varying degrees of success – deal with a 'crisis in ideology'. What do you think about this trend; do you intend to follow it through, and if so in what direction?*

I do intend to follow it through. And in fact *Theorem* does do this. . . . The point of the film is roughly this: a member of the bourgeoisie, whatever he does, is always wrong. Apart from historical errors, like the idea of the Nation, the idea of God, the idea of a confessional Church, and so on, anything done by the bourgeoisie, however sincere, profound and noble it is, is always on the wrong track. But this condemnation of the bourgeoisie which used before (which means for me up until 1967) to be absolute and inescapable has to be suspended before a final assessment is made, since the bourgeoisie is at present undergoing a change. The sort of indignation and anger against the classical bourgeoisie, as one has always thought of it, no longer has any rationale behind it because the bourgeoisie is undergoing a revolutionary change: it is assimilating everybody to the petit bourgeoisie: the whole of mankind is becoming petit bourgeois. So there are new problems, and these will have to be solved by the members of the bourgeoisie themselves, not the workers or the opposition. We dissident bourgeois cannot solve these problems, and neither can the 'natural' bourgeois. That is why the film remains 'suspended'; it ends up with a cry, and the very irrationality of this cry conveys this absence of an answer. There are certain political and ideological themes (for example, the relationship between religion and political contestation, anger against the bourgeoisie, etc. which are also features of *Uccellacci e Uccellini*), which only become clear once the film is over.

Apart from the novelty of re-creating a bourgeois atmosphere and bourgeois characters, what have you tried to do in Theorem? *In particular you have alluded to your 'reverential' attitude as an author towards people who belong to mythology or pre-history. It seems as though from* Uccellacci *onwards your existential attitude, and therefore your stylistic approach, have both been changing. What is your stylistic attitude towards the bourgeois (and therefore presumably negative) characters in* Theorem?

The shift to a bourgeois atmosphere is purely formal. I am not making a film about bourgeois manners or life-style. And, besides, these bourgeois never speak (the film is almost silent); they do not use their own expressions, they have no attitude, etc. They, too, are seen in this particular way which I call 'reverential', which is my way of looking at human beings (who, up to now, have been subproletarians). These members of the bourgeoisie are never presented in a realist or polemical light, as they are usually seen in films which set out to depict their mode of living (cf. the work of Arbasino or Cederna). If I strip the bourgeois of all that, then he appears completely naked, as what he essentially is. So what you have is characters who are fairly absolute, and who are seen in my consistently reverential and mythical way.

The central figure in Theorem – *the Terence Stamp character* – *does his authenticity represent judgment or love?*

This character has come out ambiguous, half-way between the angelic and the demoniac. The visitor is good-looking, and good, but there is something vulgar about him as well (since he, too, is a member of the bourgeoisie). There are no uncultured bourgeois who are not vulgar; only culture can purify. So there is this element of vulgarity in him, which he has accepted so as to descend among these bourgeois people, so he is ambiguous. On the other hand, what is authentic is the love that he arouses, because it is a love without any compromise, a love which provokes scandal, which destroys, which alters the bourgeois' idea of themselves; what is authentic is this love, and the cause of this love is this ambiguous person.

So there is no relation with St Matthew's Christ, your Christ?

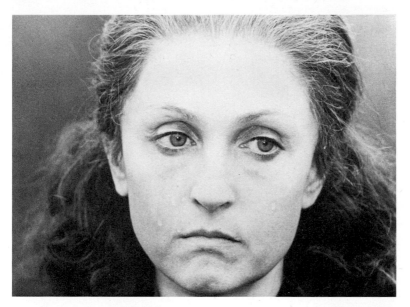

Laura Betti approaching sainthood in *Theorem*, and acting sanctity in *La Ricotta*

This character cannot be identified with Christ; rather with God, God the Father (or a messenger who represents the Father). It is an Old Testament, not a New Testament visitor.

As there is often a close connection between your cinema and your literary work, is Theorem *linked to anything you have done before? How closely is it connected with your recent literary work?*

It is curious and significant the way I got the idea for *Theorem*. About three years ago I began to write for the theatre for the first time in my life. I wrote six verse tragedies, and initially *Theorem* was supposed to be the seventh: I began working on it in the form of a verse tragedy. And then I realized that the love between the divine visitor and these bourgeois characters would be much more beautiful if it were silent. So then I began to think it might be better to make it into a film, but I could not see how to do this. So I wrote a first draft, which was very schematic, and then worked on that until I got a scenario, which I changed around and filled out, and it became a fairly autonomous literary work. So *Theorem* passed through two phases: one, a theatre piece, which was rejected; and then a second phase which had two aspects, one cinematographic and the other literary.

← *Theorem:* peasant burial preceding the miracle

Filmography

Collaboration on scenarios and scripts

1954 *La Donna del Fiume*
Director: Mario Soldati
Script: Basilio Franchina, Giorgio Bassani, Pier Paolo Pasolini, Florestano
Vancini, Antonio Altovitti and Mario Soldati
Produced by Excelsa-Carlo Ponti
Distributed by Minerva Film
With Sophia Loren

1955 *Il Prigioniero della Montagna*
Director: Luis Trenker
From the novel by C. G. Bienek
Script: Luis Trenker, Giorgio Bassani, Pier Paolo Pasolini
Produced by Bardo Film
Distribution: regional in Italy
With Marianne Hold, Luis Trenker

1956 *Le Notti di Cabiria*
Director: Federico Fellini
Subject and script: Federico Fellini, Ennio Flaiano and Tullio Pinelli
Adviser/collaborator on the script: Pier Paolo Pasolini
Produced by Dino De Laurentiis Cinematografica
Distributed by Paramount
With Giulietta Masina

1957 *Marisa La Civetta*
Director-scenarist: Mauro Bolognini
Script: Mauro Bolognini, Pier Paolo Pasolini, Titina Demby
Produced by Carlo Ponti (Rome)/Balcazar (Barcelona)
Distribution: Cei-Incom

1958 *Giovani Mariti*
Director: Mauro Bolognini
Subject: Massimo Franciosa and Pasquale Festa Campanile

Script: Enzo Curreli, Luciano Martino, Mauro Bolognini and Pier Paolo
  Pasolini
Produced by Nepi Film
Distributed by Lux Film

1959 *La Notte Brava*
  Director: Mauro Bolognini
  Subject: from *Ragazzi di vita* by Pier Paolo Pasolini
  Script: Pier Paolo Pasolini and Laurence Bost
  Produced by Antonio Cervi and Oreste Jacovoni for Ajace Film (Rome)/
    Franco-London Film (Paris)
  Distributed by Euro International Films
  With Rosanna Schiaffino, Laurent Terzieff, Jean-Claude Brialy, Franco
    Interlenghi, Antonella Lualdi, Mylène Demongeot, Elsa Martinelli

1960 *Morte di un Amico*
  Director: Franco Rossi
  Subject: Giuseppe Berto, Oreste Biancoli, Pier Paolo Pasolini, Franco
    Riganti
  Script: Franco Riganti, Ugo Guerra, Franco Rossi
  Produced by Alfredo Bini for Cino Del Duca-Arco Film-Lyre Cinémato-
    graphique
  Distributed by Cino Del Duca

  Il Bel Antonio
  Director: Mauro Bolognini
  Subject: from the novel by Vitaliano Brancati
  Script: Pier Paolo Pasolini, Gino Visentini, Mauro Bolognini
  Produced by Alfredo Bini
  Distributed by Cino Del Duca
  With Marcello Mastroianni, Claudia Cardinale

  La Canta delle Marane
  Director: Cecilia Mangini
  Story: from a chapter in *Ragazzi di vita* by Pier Paolo Pasolini
  Commentary by Pier Paolo Pasolini
  Produced by Giorgio Patara

  La Giornata Balorda
  Director: Mauro Bolognini
  Subject: Pier Paolo Pasolini and Alberto Moravia from *Racconti Romani*
    and *Nuovi Racconti Romani* by Alberto Moravia
  Script: Pier Paolo Pasolini, Alberto Moravia and Mario Visconti
  Produced by Paul Graetz for Produzioni Intercontinentali
  Distributed by Euro International Films

  La Lunga Notte del '43
  Director: Florestano Vancini

Subject: from the story *Una notte del '43* (part of the cycle *Le Storie Ferraresi*) by Giorgio Bassani
Script: Ennio De Concini, Pier Paolo Pasolini, Florestano Vancini

Produced by Antonio Cervi and Alessandro Jacovoni for Ajace Film-Euro International Films
Distributed by Euro International Films

Il Carro Armato dell'8 Settembre
Director: Gianni Puccini
Subject: Rodolfo Sonego, Tonino Guerra, Elio Petri
Script: Gianni Puccini Baratti, Elio Bartolini, Pier Paolo Pasolini, Giulio Questi
Produced by Film Napoleon
Distributed by Euro International Films

1961 *La Ragazza in Vetrina*
Director: Luciano Emmer
Subject: Emanuele Cassuto, Luciano Emmer, Rodolfo Sonego
Script: Luciano Emmer, Pier Paolo Pasolini, Luciano Martino, Vincio Marinucci
Produced by Nepi Film-Sofidetip-Zodiaque
Distributed by Lux Film

1962 *Una Vita Violenta*
Directors: Paolo Heusch and Brunello Rondi
Subject: from the novel *Una Vita Violenta* by Pier Paolo Pasolini
Treatment: Ennio De Concini and Franco Brusati
Script: Paolo Heusch, Brunello Rondi, Franco Solinas
Produced by Zebra Film (Rome)/Aera Films (Paris)
Distribution: Variety

La Commare Secca
Director: Bernardo Bertolucci
Subject: from a story by Pier Paolo Pasolini
Script: Bernardo Bertolucci and Sergio Citti
Produced by Antonio Cervi for the Compagnia Cinematografica Cervi-Cineriz
Distribution: Cineriz

Acted in

1960 *Il Gobbo*
    Director: Carlo Lizzani
1966 *Requiescant*
    Director: Carlo Lizzani

Directed
Accattone (1961)

Production Company	Arco Film-Cino Del Duca
Producer	Alfredo Bini
Director	Pier Paolo Pasolini
Script	Pier Paolo Pasolini
Assistant Directors	Bernardo Bertolucci, Leopoldo Savona
Assistant for Script	Sergio Citti
Director of Photography	Tonino Delli Colli
Editor	Nino Baragli
Music	Johann Sebastian Bach, co-ordinated by Carlo Rustichelli

Franco Citti (*Accattone*), Franca Pasut (*Stella*), Silvana Corsini (*Maddalena*), Paola Guidi (*Ascenza*), Adriana Asti (*Amore*)

Location: Rome
Running time: 120 mins (115 mins in Britain)
Distributors: Cino Del Duca (Italy), Connoisseur (G.B.)
Shown in Britain in 1962; not yet shown commercially in U.S.A.

Mamma Roma (1962)

Production Company	Arco Film-Cineriz
Producer	Alfredo Bini
Director	Pier Paolo Pasolini
Script	Pier Paolo Pasolini
Assistant for Script	Sergio Citti
Director of Photography	Tonino Delli Colli
Editor	Nino Baragli
Music	Vivaldi, co-ordinated by Carlo Rustichelli

Anna Magnani (*Mamma Roma*), Ettore Garofolo (*Ettore*), Franco Citti (*Carmine*), Silvana Corsini (*Bruna*), Luisa Loiano (*Biancofiore*), Paolo Volponi (*Priest*), Luciano Gonini (*Zacaria*), Vittorio La Paglia (*Signor Pellissier*), Piero Morgia (*Piero*)

Location: Rome
Running time: 110 mins (106 mins in Britain)
Distributors: Cineriz (Italy), Gala (G.B.)
Shown in Britain in 1964; not yet shown commercially in U.S.A.

La Ricotta (1962)
(episode in *Rogopag* or *Laviamoci il Cervello*; other episodes directed by Rossellini, Godard and Gregoretti).

Production Companies	Arco Film-Cineriz (Rome) and Lyre (Paris)
Director	Pier Paolo Pasolini
Subject and Script	Pier Paolo Pasolini
Director of Photography	Tonino Delli Colli
Costumes	Danilo Donati
Musical co-ordinator	Carlo Rustichelli

Orson Welles (*The Director*), Mario Cipriani (*Stracci*), Laura Betti (*The Star*), Edmonda Aldini (*Another Star*), Vittorio La Paglia (*The Journalist*), Ettore Garofolo (*An Extra*), Maria Bernardini (*Extra who does Striptease*)

Running time: 40 mins
Distributor: Cineriz (Italy)
Shown in U.S.A. in 1963; not yet shown commercially in Britain
At first banned in Italy because of the Pasolini episode, *Rogopag* was re-released under the new title of LAVIAMOCI IL CERVELLO, with some cuts in *La Ricotta* (see p. 64)

La Rabbia (1963) First part
(Second part by Giovanni Guareschi)

Producer	Gastone Ferrante
Production Company	Opus Film
Director	Pier Paolo Pasolini
Script	Pier Paolo Pasolini
Commentary spoken by	Giorgio Bassani, Renato Guttuso
Editor	Nino Baragli

Running time: 50 mins
Distributor: Warner Bros
The film was withdrawn by Warners immediately because of Guareschi's episode and has never been commercially released anywhere since (see p. 72)

Sopraluoghi in Palestina per 'Il Vangelo Secondo Matteo' (1963–64)

Production Company	Arco Film
Cameraman	Aldo Pennelli
Speakers	Pier Paolo Pasolini, Don Andrea Carraro
Commentary	Pier Paolo Pasolini

Running time: 50 mins
Never distributed commercially anywhere
Edited and commented by Pasolini for the VIII Spoleto Festival, July 1965
For the conditions in which this was done see p. 73f.

Comizi d'Amore (1964)

Production Company	Arco Film
Producer	Alfredo Bini
Production Manager	Eliseo Boschi
Director	Pier Paolo Pasolini
Commentary written by	Pier Paolo Pasolini
Commentary spoken by	Lello Bersani and Pier Paolo Pasolini
Participants	Pier Paolo Pasolini, Cesare Musatti, Giuseppe Ungaretti, Susanna Pasolini, Camilla Cederna, Adele Cambria, Oriana Fallaci, Antonella Lualdi, Graziella Granata (and, suppressed in the editing, Giuseppe Ravegnani and Eugenio Montale)
Directors of Photography	Mario Bernardo, Tonino Delli Colli
Camera Operators	Vittorio Bernini, Franco Delli Colli, Cesare Fontana
Editor	Nino Baragli

Locations: Palermo, Calabria, Naples, the Po Valley and various sites throughout Italy
Running time: 90 mins
Distributor: Titanus (Italy)
Not yet shown commercially in Britain or U.S.A.

Il Vangelo Secondo Matteo (1964)

Production Companies	Arco Film (Rome), Lux Cie Cinématographique de France (Paris)
Producer	Alfredo Bini
Production Manager	Eliseo Boschi
Director	Pier Paolo Pasolini
Director of Photography	Tonino Delli Colli
Camera Operator	Giuseppe Ruzzolini
Editor	Nino Baragli
Music	Johann Sebastian Bach, Wolfgang Amadeus Mozart, Sergei Prokofiev, Anton Webern, Luis E. Bacalov
Costumes	Danilo Donati
Sound	Mario Del Pezzo

Enrique Irazoqui (*Christ*), Margherita Caruso (*The Young Mary*), Susanna Pasolini (*The Old Mary*), Marcello Morante (*Joseph*), Mario Socrate (*John The Baptist*), Settimio Di Porto (*Peter*), Otello Sestili (*Judas*), Ferruccio Nuzzo (*Matthew*), Giacomo Morante (*John*), Alfonso Gatto (*Andrew*), Enzo Siciliano (*Simon*), Giorgio Agamben (*Philip*), Guido Cerretani (*Bartholomew*), Luigi

Barbini (*James, the Son of Alphaeus*), Marcello Galdini (*James, the Son of Zebedee*), Elio Spaziani (*Thaddeus*), Rosario Migale (*Thomas*), Rodolfo Wilcock (*Caiphas*), Alessandro Clerici (*Pontius Pilate*), Amerigo Bevilacqua (*Herod I*), Francesco Leonetti (*Herod II*), Paola Tedesco (*Salome*), Rossana di Rocco (*Angel*), Eliseo Boschi (*Joseph of Aramathea*), Natalia Ginzburg (*Mary of Bethany*)

Locations in Southern Italy (Calabria, Lucania, Puglie)
Running time: 140 mins (135 mins in Britain)
Distributors: Titanus (Italy), Compton (G.B.), Continental (U.S.A.)
Shown in U.S.A. in 1964 and in Britain in 1967, title THE GOSPEL ACCORDING TO ST MATTHEW
The word 'St' was introduced against Pasolini's express wishes into the English title. The dedication to John XXIII was likewise truncated in English
Christ's voice: Enrico Maria Salerno

Uccellacci e Uccellini (1966)

Production Company	Arco Film
Producer	Alfredo Bini
Production Manager	Fernando Franchi
Director	Pier Paolo Pasolini
Assistant Director	Sergio Citti
Script	Pier Paolo Pasolini
Directors of Photography	Mario Bernardo, Tonino Delli Colli
Camera Operators	Franco Di Giacomo, Gaetano Valle
Editor	Nino Baragli
Music	Ennio Morricone
Costumes	Danilo Donati
Sound	Pietro Ortolani

Totò (*Innocenti Totò and Brother Ciccillo*), Ninetto Davoli (*Innocenti Ninetto and Brother Ninetto*), Femi Benussi (*Luna*), Rossana Di Rocco (*Friend of Ninetto*), Lena Lin Solaro (*Urganda La Sconosciuta*), Rosina Moroni (*Peasant Woman*), Renato Capogna and Pietro Davoli (*Medieval Louts*), Gabriele Baldini (*Dante's Dentist*), Riccardo Redi (*Ingegnere*)

Filmed on location around Rome – at Tuscania, near Fiumicino, near the EUR, and various other places
Running time: 86 mins
Distributor: Marchio (Italy)
Not yet shown commercially in Britain. Released in the U.S.A. in 1966, title THE HAWKS AND THE SPARROWS
The crow's voice is that of Francesco Leonetti

Le Streghe (1966)

(episode *La Terra vista dalla Luna*)
Other episodes by Luchino Visconti, Mauro Bolognini, Franco Rossi,
Vittorio De Sica

Production Company	Dino De Laurentiis Cinematografica
Director	Pier Paolo Pasolini
Script	Pier Paolo Pasolini
Director of Photography	Giuseppe Rotunno
Colour Process	Technicolor
Costumes	Piero Tosi
Sculptures	Pino Zac
Editor	Piero Piccioni
Assistant Director	Sergio Citti

Totò (*Ciancicato Miao*), Ninetto Davoli (*Basciù Miao*), Silvana Mangano
(*Assurdina Caì*), Laura Betti (*Tourist*), Luigi Leone (*Tourist's Wife*), Mario
Cipriani (*Priest*)

Location: Rome and surroundings (Fiumicino)
Distribution: Dear Film/United Artists (Italy), Lopert (U.S.A.)
Shown in U.S.A. in 1969; not yet shown commercially in Britain

Capriccio all'Italiana (1966)

(episode *Che Cosa Sono le Nuvole?*)
Other episodes by Steno, Mauro Bolognini (2), Pino Zac, Mario
Monicelli

Production Company	Dino De Laurentiis Cinematografica
Producer	Dino De Laurentiis
Director	Pier Paolo Pasolini
Script	Pier Paolo Pasolini
Director of Photography	Tonino Delli Colli
Editor	Nino Baragli
Song: 'Così sono le Nuvole'	Domenico Modugno and Pier Paolo Pasolini
Colour Process	Technicolor

Totò (*Iago*), Franco Franchi (*Cassio*), Ciccio Ingrassia (*Roderigo*), Domenico
Modugno (*Dustman*), Ninetto Davoli (*Othello*), Laura Betti (*Desdemona*),
Adriana Asti (*Bianca*), Carlo Pisacane (*Brabantio*), Francesco Leonetti (*Puppeteer*)

Distributors: Euro International Films (Italy)
Not yet shown commercially in Britain or U.S.A.

Edipo Re (1967)

Production Company	Arco Film
Producer	Alfredo Bini
Production Manager	Eliseo Boschi
Director	Pier Paolo Pasolini
Script	Pier Paolo Pasolini, inspired by *Oedipus Rex* and *Oedipus at Colonus* by Sophocles
Director of Photography	Giuseppe Ruzzolini
Camera Operator	Otello Spila
Assistant Director	Jean-Claude Biette
Editor	Nino Baragli
Music	Rumanian and Japanese folk-music, plus original music co-ordinated by Pier Paolo Pasolini
Costumes	Danilo Donati

Franco Citti (*Oedipus*), Silvana Mangano (*Jocasta*), Alida Villa (*Merope*), Carmelo Bene (*Creon*), Julian Beck (*Tiresias*), Luciano Bartoli (*Laius*), Francesco Leonetti (*Servant*), Ahmed Bellashmi (*Polybus*), Giandomenico Davoli (*Shepherd of Polybus*), Ninetto Davoli (*Messenger*), Pier Paolo Pasolini (*High Priest*), Jean-Claude Biette (*Priest*)

Shot in Northern Italy, Morocco and Bologna
Running time: 110 mins (104 mins in Britain)
Distributors: Euro International Films (Italy), Eagle (G.B.)
Shown in Britain in 1969, entitled OEDIPUS REX

Amore e Rabbia (1967)
(episode *La Fiore di Campo*)
Other episodes directed by Lizziani, Bertolucci, Godard, Bellocchio

Production Company	Castoro Film (Rome) Anouchka Film (Paris)
Director	Pier Paolo Pasolini
Director of Photography	Guiseppe Ruzzolini
Colour Process	Technicolor
Music	Giovanni Fusco; J. S. Bach: St Matthew Passion

With Ninetto Davoli

Shot in Rome (Via Nazionale)
Running time: 12 mins

Teorema (1968)

Production Company	Aetos Film
Producers	Franco Rossellini, Manolo Bolognini

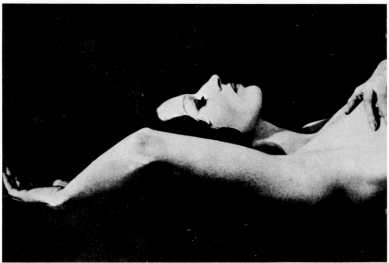

Maria Callas in *Medea*; Silvana Mangano in *Theorem*

Production Manager	Paolo Frascà
Director	Pier Paolo Pasolini
Assistant Director	Sergio Citti
Script	Pier Paolo Pasolini, based on his own novel
Director of Photography	Giuseppe Ruzzolini
Colour Process	Eastman Colour
Editor	Nino Baragli
Music	Ennio Morricone
Musical Director	Bruno Nicolai
Sound	Dario Fronzetti

Terence Stamp (*The Visitor*), Silvana Mangano (*Lucia*), Massimo Girotti (*Paolo*), Anne Wiazemsky (*Odetta*), Laura Betti (*Emilia*), Andrès José Cruz (*Pietro*), Ninetto Davoli (*Angelino*), Alfonso Gatto, Carlo De Mejo, Adele Cambria

Running time: 98 mins
Distributors: Euro International Films (Italy), Eagle (G.B.)
Shown in Britain in 1969, title THEOREM

Il Porcile (1969)

Production Company	Film dell'Orso
Director	Pier Paolo Pasolini

With Ugo Tognazzi, Jean-Pierre Léaud, Pierre Clementi, Anne Wiazemski, Franco Citti

Medea (1969)

Production Company	San Marco
Producer	Franco Rossellini
Script	Pier Paolo Pasolini from *Medea* by Euripides

With Maria Callas and Guiseppe Gentile

Shot on location in Turkey
Distributors: Euro International Films (Italy)

Bibliography

Books by Pasolini

Poesia dialettale del Novecento, Parma, Guanda, 1952.

La meglio gioventù, poesie friulane, Florence, Sansoni, 1954.

Canzoniere italiano, antologia della poesia popolare, Parma, Guanda, 1955.

Ragazzi di Vita, Milan, Garzanti, 1955.

Le ceneri di Gramsci, Milan, Garzanti, 1957.

L'usignolo della Chiesa Cattolica, Milan, Longanesi, 1958.

Una vita violenta, Milan, Garzanti, 1959. English translation: *A Violent Life*, London, Cape, 1968.

Sonetto primaverile, Milan, Scheiwiller, 1960.

Donne di Roma, introduction by Alberto Moravia, Milan, Il Saggiatore, 1960.

Roma 1950, diario, Milan, Scheiwiller, 1960.

La poesia popolare italiana, Milan, Garzanti, 1960.

Passione e ideologia, Milan, Garzanti, 1960.

Come è nato l'universo, Roma, Citta Nuova, 1961.

La religione del nostro tempo, Milan, Garzanti, 1961.

La Commare Secca, Milan, Zibetti, 1962 (with Bernardo Bertolucci).

Accattone, Rome, Edizioni FN, 1961.

Mamma Roma, Milan, Rizzoli, 1962.

L'odore dell'India, Milan, Longanesi, 1962.

Il sogno di una cosa, Milan, Garzanti, 1963.

Il Vangelo secondo Matteo, Milan, Garzanti, 1964.

Poesia in forma di rosa, Milan, Garzanti, 1964.

Alì Dagli Occhi Azzurri, Milan, Garzanti, 1965.

Uccellacci e Uccellini, Milan, Garzanti, 1966.

Edipo Re, Milan, Garzanti, 1967.

Teorema, Milan, Garzanti, 1968.

Translation: *Il Vantone* (from Plautus' *Miles Gloriosus*), Milan, Garzanti.

Articles on Cinema

'Nuove Questioni Linguistiche' ['*New Linguistic Questions*'], *Rinascita* 51, 1964.

'Diario Linguistico' ['Linguistic Diary'], *Rinascita* 10, 1965.

'Il Cinema di Poesia' ['The Cinema of Poetry']: originally a paper delivered by Pasolini at the Pesaro Festival in June 1965; it is reprinted in full in the volume of *Uccellacci e Uccellini* and, slightly truncated, in *Filmcritica* 156–7; it has been translated into English in *Cahiers du Cinéma in English* 6. Pasolini's interview in *Cahiers de Cinéma* 169 (in French), is an essential adjunct to this text.

'In Calce al "Cinema di Poesia"' ['Footnote to "The Cinema of Poetry"'], *Filmcritica* 163.

'Laboratorio' [Laboratory], *Nuovi Argomenti* 1 (nuova serie): this text has two parts, the first entitled 'Appunti *en poète* per una linguistica marxista' [Notes written *en poète* for a Marxist Linguistics] and the second: 'La sceneggiatura come struttura che vuol essere altra struttura' ['The scenario as a structure designed to become another structure']. The second text is reprinted in the volume of *Uccellacci e Uccellini* and is also translated into French in *Cahiers du Cinéma* 185.

'La Lingua Scritta dell'Azione' ['The Written Language of Action'], *Nuovi Argomenti* 2 (nuova serie): Pasolini's paper at the 1966 Pesaro Festival.

'La Fine dell'Avanguardia' ['The End of the Avant Garde'], *Nuovi Argomenti* 3–4: this text demands an acquaintance with Roland Barthes's interview in *Cahiers du Cinéma* 147 (reprinted in Italian in *Cinema e Film* 1).

'Dialogo 1', *Cinema e Film* 1 (series of talks between Pasolini and two of the editors of *Cinema e Film* written out by Pasolini as a continuous text).

'La Paura del Naturalismo (Osservazioni sul piano-sequenza)' ['The Fear of Naturalism (Observations on the Long Take)'], *Nuovi Argomenti* 6: the text of Pasolini's talk at the 1967 Pesaro Festival.

'Sintagmi Viventi e Poeti Morti' ['Living Syntagms and Dead Poets'], *Rinascita* 33, 1967.

About Pasolini

There is a detailed bibliography of Pasolini's works and commentaries on them in Gian Carlo Ferretti, *Letteratura e ideologia*, Rome, 1964. Cf. B.F.I. Book Library Bibliography no. 21.

The two most enlightening discussions of Pasolini as a writer are by Franco Fortini, 'Le poesie italiane di questi anni', *Il Menabò* 2 (1960) and Alberto Asor Rosa, *Scrittori e popolo*, Rome, 1965.

There is very little material by or about Pasolini in English. The only one of his works translated into English is *Una vita violenta* [*A Violent Life*], Cape, 1968. A few of his poems have been translated in anthologies. The following texts are available concerning the cinema:

1. 'Intellectualism . . . and the Teds', *Films and Filming*, January 1961.

2. 'Cinematic and Literary Stylistic Figures', *Film Culture* 24 (spring 1962).

3. *The New York Herald Tribune* of 22 November 1964 contains an interview with Pasolini, by Sanche de Gramont.

4. *Film Quarterly*, vol. 18, no. 4 (summer 1965): Pasolini at the Rome Film School, a shortened version of the text in *Bianco e Nero* 6, 1964.

5. *Film Comment*, Fall 1965 contains an introductory article on Pasolini by GH (= Gordon Hitchens), an article by Maryvonne Butcher, the film critic of *The Tablet* (condensed from *Christian Communications*, 13 July 1965), a translation of Pasolini's poem on the death of Pope Pius XII (originally in *Officina*, now in *Religione del mio tempo*) and an interview with Pasolini, by James Blue (the director of *Les Oliviers de la Justice*).

6. *Cahiers du Cinéma in English* 6 contains a shortened version of 'The Cinema of Poetry'.

7. *Film Culture*, Fall 1966 contains a discussion between Pasolini, Varda, Allio, Sarris and Michelson and an account of a Press conference given by Pasolini at the 1966 New York Film Festival.

8. *Arts in Society*, vol. 4, no. 1 (winter 1966/7): Pasolini's answers to a questionnaire.

9. *Cinema* 3 contains an audacious article on *Theorem* by Mike Wallington.

Acknowledgements

Particular thanks go to Camillo Pennati of the Italian Institute in London, a gracious source of wisdom and knowledge; to Walter Cantatore of Arco Film, Rome, who arranged for me to see several films and gave generously of his time to assist in the project; to Fiorella A. for logistical aid; to B.B.C. *Release* and *Inquadrature*, Pavia, for allowing me to reprint sections of interviews on *Theorem*; to the staff of the B.F.I. for setting up the book and enabling me to see some of Pasolini's films in London; and lastly to Pier Paolo Pasolini who took a sizeable amount of time off his heavy work schedule during the editing of *Theorem* to do these interviews. One film company was distinctly unhelpful: as they no doubt know who they are, let them here find this expression of my sincere loathing.

Stills are reproduced by courtesy of Arco Film, Dino De Laurentiis Cinematografica, Euro International Films, Eagle Films, *L'Astrolabio*, Ullstein Bilderdienst, the Danish Embassy in London and the Radio Times Hulton Picture Library. The still of *Medea* is from a photograph by Christopher Martin.

O.S.